GRACE TAYLOR

ACCELERATED LEARNING STRATEGIES

Master Your Mind, Master Your Life
(2024 Guide for Beginners)

Copyright © 2024 by GRACE TAYLOR

All rights reserved. No part of this publication may be reproduced, stored or transmitted in any form or by any means, electronic, mechanical, photocopying, recording, scanning, or otherwise without written permission from the publisher. It is illegal to copy this book, post it to a website, or distribute it by any other means without permission.

First edition

This book was professionally typeset on Reedsy.
Find out more at reedsy.com

Contents

1. CHAPTER 1: HOW TO STUDY EFFECTIVELY — 1
2. CHAPTER 2: STUDYING STRATEGIES — 13
3. CHAPTER 3: IMPORTANT STUDY TACTICS — 34
4. CHAPTER 4: TEN EFFECTIVE TIPS AND HACKS TO SAVE YOUR TIME... — 50
5. CHAPTER 5: STUDY HABITS — 72
6. CHAPTER 6: CONCENTRATION AND STUDYING — 91
7. CHAPTER 7: CREATING AND MAINTAINING A STUDY LEARNING CULTURE — 99
8. CHAPTER 8: CONTINUOUS LEARNING DEVELOPMENT — 108
9. CHAPTER 9: LEARNING THE BASICS — 119
10. CHAPTER 10: READING SPEED — 138
11. CHAPTER 11: VISUALIZATION AND CONCEPTUALIZATION — 154
12. CHAPTER 12: COMPREHENSION — 168
13. CHAPTER 13: SPEED WRITING SKILLS — 186
14. CHAPTER 14: WRITING FOR STUDY — 201
15. CHAPTER 15: SPEEDWRITING FOR FASTER NOTE-TAKING — 216
16. CHAPTER 16: WRITING SPECIFIC DOCUMENTS — 226

1

CHAPTER 1: HOW TO STUDY EFFECTIVELY

Even if someone may be studying for lengthy periods of time, does this imply that they are understanding the material? For decades, scientists have struggled in this field.

But most educational establishments hardly ever succeed in imparting this essential knowledge. Consequently, letting the pupils fend for themselves. The prerequisite environment for successful study will be thoroughly covered in Chapter 1. These study spaces offer useful suggestions that you should give a try the next time you have some important studying to accomplish. As previously mentioned, each person has a different ideal study location, so it's best to experiment with these suggestions until you find one that suits you.

Proper Conditions to Learning

The first step is to identify your most comfortable location. While some people require background noise, others would rather be alone. If you can work best in an environment with some background noise, you might choose to visit a coffee shop or an open park; for those who need complete quiet, a library might be the ideal choice. Second, a recommended lighting system should preferably be present in the study space chosen. Dim lighting is more likely to cause fatigue and impair attention more quickly. Effective studying occurs when one is most productive, which is also the optimum moment. Just because it suits your close study partner doesn't mean that one should wake up early to study.

In order to study well, one needs also be cautious of situations or surroundings that deplete energy and cause distraction. Social media is one of the biggest obstacles to paying close attention. It is advisable to shut down all social media accounts and turn off the internet in order to focus on your studies. Turning off electronics like cellphones is also advised because they have the potential to become addicting. Incoming call and message answering results in the loss of valuable study time and focus. Ultimately, it's probable that fatigue will set in before any real learning is accomplished. Lack of concentration from intense studying may also be caused by other distractions, such as studying when the television is on.

Public libraries and campuses are obvious options. Here, it's critical to recognize that each person has unique tastes. Being aware of and reducing your distractions can enable you to concentrate on your task. It's a good idea to try out different background noises and settings until you discover the ideal blend.

Creating a routine that signals to your brain that it is time to start working can help you accomplish the task at hand, regardless of the kind of setting you are in. while you enable quicker shifts while switching between tasks, our minds may find it difficult to adjust. A habit that has been established over time might aid with focus.

At times, the ideal setting has less to do with your study

location and more to do with the individuals in your immediate vicinity. Therefore, asking for help from others may be the perfect way to encourage more gregarious kids to focus on their studies. Study groups, whether official or informal, may provide a great forum for idea exchange and generally improve mutual learning. These study sessions and groups also help people become more accountable to the greater group, which improves their capacity to learn. It's also possible to adopt the position of "teacher" and provide other study participants with an intensive introduction to the material. Another efficient technique to absorb the information is to explain it to someone else.

How to Set Up for Success

Academic success is contingent upon several elements, all of which are under the learner's control. The most successful students know how to prioritize their academics while making time for extracurricular activities, friends, and family. They are excellent time managers because they adhere to reasonable study plans and maximize classroom effectiveness. These kids know how to have fun on campus or at school even as they concentrate on learning new things and doing well in their classes.

Success and prioritizing your education are highly correlated. When presented with the option to attend a lavish party or study for a test, a successful student selects the latter. In order to catch up with their academics, those who are falling behind in a specific difficult topic choose to forgo their favorite humor.

Another essential component of success is operating with integrity. implying that one should work independently and abstain from lying. Students at certain universities develop a group mindset that undermines their ethical practices since they are accustomed to dishonesty.

Such immoral characteristics might trick a student into believing that it is beneficial to cut corners in their education, but in the long run, it always results in some bad habits that contribute to failed professions.

Another important factor in their performance is that they are maintaining their attention on the current study assignments. An attentive learner begins by conditioning their mind to focus for extended periods of time. Eventually, they will be able to dedicate themselves to a work for up to ninety minutes. This method develops the uncommon habit of committing oneself fully to a task until it is completed. Making a plan for every study session is another strategy for maintaining concentration to achieve objectives and guarantee good output. A good learner also understands that gradual advancement has greater significance than instantaneous and extraordinary solutions. Rather of jumping right into the finished result, these learners will want to concentrate on the intricacies.

Participation guarantees achievement by fostering positive relationships with peers and teachers. Students who actively participate in class discussions and make an attempt to contribute are more likely to benefit from the classroom learning environment.

The Necessity of Resource Analysis

Participation guarantees achievement by fostering positive relationships with peers and teachers. Students who actively participate in class discussions and make an attempt to contribute are more likely to benefit from the classroom learning environment.

Academic texts are not the sole main sources of knowledge used in formal education or study. Additional useful resources should be included as well, including periodicals, radio and television shows, documentaries, and the internet. In terms of common sourcebooks, some different genres or sorts include encyclopedias, yearbooks, biographies, and preserved documents; they are all either non-fiction or fiction. There are other categories for online resources, but the most important thing to remember is that a source's applicability will vary depending on the topic of the study or research the student is working on. Since each source will have a different level of authenticity, it is also essential to utilize one's judgment while selecting sources.

Resources for studying or learning are now divided into many categories. It is crucial to look over this as soon as possible and assess how it affects learning effectiveness. The resources we take from primary sources make reference to a particular event or study era. Literary writings, speeches, letters, and historical diaries are a few examples of these primary materials. Conversely, secondary sources can be found after an event has occurred because the author was most likely not there for the game or related events. Usually, these texts make an effort to offer an interpretation. A great example of secondary resources are a variety of scholarly texts. The term "tertiary documents" refers to a last category of documents that comprise directories, bibliographies, and indexes.

When considering the sources from which a student should obtain knowledge, it is useful to remember that there are several options. Nonetheless, libraries would be the main source. Most usually, a college or university's official library, replete with a document retrieval system, is available to its students. The computer can be used to access these systems. These papers are accessible online in the majority of these educational institutions.

These make sure that information is always available, not just while the library is open but also anywhere there is an internet connection. Multiple students can access the content simultaneously using such a setup. In addition, the internet is renowned for being a remarkable source.

Regardless of the source of knowledge, adherence to academic norms and regulations is crucial. When it comes to books and journals, a diligent student is especially careful to cite the page numbers when they plan to choose and utilize a quotation or paraphrase from a work.

Students who want to cite or use the web pages as source material must have access to the web URLs as well as information about the date of access. Since plagiarism is a severe academic infraction, correct reference must always be followed.

CHAPTER 1: HOW TO STUDY EFFECTIVELY

Strategies for Creating a Study Plan

Developing a successful study schedule helps pupils become autonomous and self-motivated. A goal plan of this kind guarantees that the student develops into a focused learner who takes responsibility for their education, successfully manages their time, breaks bad habits like procrastination, leads a balanced life, and routinely performs well in their studies. Setting up both long- and short-term goals is the first step in creating a successful strategy. The goals outline aids in identifying the areas that require serious study hours and concentration. Short-term objectives may include practicing for a PowerPoint presentation that is due in 14 days, finishing a term paper in three weeks, or performing well on a test that is due in two weeks. To make them easier to handle, they should be divided into weeks or months. To better understand what has to be done, the next step is to put all of the responsibilities on paper. All of the courses and disciplines that a student has to study for at a certain moment may be on the list. Subsequently, a precise plan outlining the requirements for each class must be implemented. It's possible that the level of dedication needed for one session will change from another. Set aside time for reading, going over notes, and creating study aids for each of these courses. The next crucial stage is to rank each recognized course.

Following the creation of a priority list, the student divides the whole amount of time available each week into study blocks. Certain courses or disciplines may be allocated to these blocks. Students need to make sure they set aside time for hobbies, family, and friends in order to have balanced lives. It's critical to strike a healthy balance between your personal and academic lives. It's time to fill up the schedule now, indicating which specific subject will be covered in each session. This helps the student stay on course, establishes benchmarks for the content, and makes it possible to arrange the resources needed for study in advance.

The timetable that is designed must consider the personality of the student by assessing their time management skills in a realistic manner, assisting in determining which areas they can be more efficient in and which additional activities would burden them. Determining one's learning style might also help in identifying any activity overlaps. Additionally, it will assist a student in learning how to make the most of the time they do not spend effectively. Here, the important things to consider are if you are an auditory learner who finds it easier to study while driving by listening to lectures that have been recorded or other audio content. On the other hand, a visual learner is someone who learns best via watching movies or watching videos. It's also critical to pause and consider one's work ethic.

Positive Mindset for Effective Studies

A student's life both inside and outside of the classroom can be significantly impacted by a fundamentally optimistic outlook. Students still need to know how to acquire and use the talent of positive thinking on a regular basis, though. This is due to the fact that students face a variety of difficulties each and every day of their academic careers. They are constantly challenged to go above and beyond what they can do in order to learn new things and gain new talents. It takes a lot of strength and resolve to do all of this. When faced with enormous problems, most students feel dread, discouragement, or a sense of giving up if they don't have an optimistic mindset and trust in their skills.

Lack of positive thinking is seen in students who are uncomfortable asking for help, who routinely fail to finish tasks, and who forget to turn in their homework. Psychologically speaking, our behaviors have an impact on our feelings. Positive emotions increase the likelihood that students will feel confident in their work. On the other hand, pessimistic views increase the likelihood of feeling overwhelmed and decrease the likelihood of acting. Therefore, starting to study, turning in assignments, and generally organizing their study time is one method for students who want to be competent to show that they have a positive outlook.

Additionally, there is a cognitive pattern that students ought to adopt. That belief gives rise to thoughts, which in turn give rise to feelings, which give rise to deeds, which give rise to consequences. Put another way, our beliefs determine the results we get, like the grades we get. Thus, pupils who have authority over their beliefs and ideas also have authority over the outcomes that result from those beliefs and ideas. A student who thinks they can succeed in physics will think the subject is manageable. After that, the pupils would feel and become more certain while approaching this subject. They will most likely do well on any given physics task as a result of this feeling. With all of that, the pupils will undoubtedly receive high grades.

Teachers may help students by finding out how they feel about their studies and paying close attention to any views they may have, whether good or negative. In the event that the instructor notices a student talking poorly about their efforts, they may be urged to rephrase their descriptions to sound more optimistic. After that, the student can talk about steps that can be made to resolve the issue in a way that is beneficial. When faced with situations that require resolution, it is critical to have faith in the student's capacity for innovative problem-solving.

This is connected to the law of cause and effect, which says that the seeds sowed are what yield the desired effects. The fruits of previous deeds are results.

Consequently, it is possible to understand a student's current circumstances in light of recent events. If students adhere to this fundamental idea, they may take charge of their education and future professions. A student must consistently study and seek assistance when needed if they hope to perform well on their tests. Students must sit down and do their assignments if they hope to finish them. Students are constantly challenged to improve beyond their existing talents, as I mentioned previously.

As such, they must plant personal "seeds of approach" and "seeds of habit" that will benefit them in the long run. It is advised to plant "seeds of habit" such as diligence, regular study sessions, a schedule for completing schoolwork, asking for assistance when necessary, and turning in assignments on time. The traits that are suggested as "seeds of approach" are being receptive to new information, having optimism about education and opportunities in the future, being supportive of oneself and others, confidently taking constructive criticism, and being kind and courteous to parents, instructors, and other students. Because our thoughts eventually shape who we are.

2

CHAPTER 2: STUDYING STRATEGIES

Students might find studying to be both enjoyable and beneficial. This is only feasible, though, if efficient study techniques are applied to prevent pupils from becoming disinterested and giving up. The chapter discusses a number of tried-and-true methods and pointers that can help ensure that the experience is both pleasurable and fruitful.

Elaborative Interrogation

Using this method, the student reads the information that has to be recalled and comes up with an explanation. The learner utilizes inquiries like "how" and "why" to decipher the significance of the material. During the active learning process, it helps to improve memory. Using this method, teachers urge students to come up with potential solutions that clarify the cause-and-effect link between a subject and the predicate. Put another way, it includes drawing connections between concepts that a student is learning and then relating the information to personal experiences and day-to-day activities. The learner can consider the connections between several concepts and comprehend how they differ or are similar to one another.

After questions are created, students must sort through their prior knowledge to see if they can make a link between the new and old material that is at their disposal in order to answer the questions that are provided to them. In order to get hints to answer the questions, students must use their past knowledge and critically evaluate or reflect on their readings. When employing this strategy, educators should first demonstrate how to formulate a why inquiry following reading a statement. After that, there is an open discussion in class during which students provide potential responses to the questions. Following their compilation, students continue to debate which option best addresses the topic. Assign the students to create questions and answers related to the material they will be learning in groups. They are urged to read the content and search for hints to help them answer the specific questions at this phase. After that, they must come up with potential responses on their own. Reminding them that there is no right or incorrect response in this learning process is necessary.

The pupils will eventually absorb the technique and even be able to formulate the questions and come up with the answers on their own. By continuously creating new connections and details, the major objective is for the pupils to comprehend better concepts, their relationships, and how they differ from one another.

A real-world illustration would come from a historical occasion, such as the attack on Pearl Harbor. An astute history student could wonder, "Why did the attack happen?" The Japanese intended to eliminate the US Pacific Fleet in order to prevent it from interfering with their activities. "What was the result of this historic attack?" would be a good follow up query. That being said, 2,400 Americans lost their lives and 1,100 were wounded.

Conversely, Japanese casualties were quite minimal. The US Navy lost eight ships, and so on. An additional query would be, "What made the attack significant?" Following the delivery of his famous speech, then-President Delano Roosevelt ordered the internment of Japanese Americans in camps.

Self-Explanation

This method of thinking aloud is well-known. Inquiring further helps the student comprehend what their brain is doing. This occurs when a student works through a difficulty that forces them to become aware of the mental processes they are going through. The learner poses inquiries, works with others to brainstorm precise solutions, tries an alternative technique, notes errors, recognizes shifts in strategy, and so on. As the name suggests, the student describes to themselves what they are doing and thinking while keeping an eye on the problem-solving process.

When the learning effects of several tactics are compared, the self-explain strategy performs better than teacher explanation. In addition, it requires a lot less time than other study methods like taking notes, summarizing, thinking aloud, or working through additional issues. During this process, the learner also becomes aware of their ignorance, which helps them to fill in the gaps in knowledge, assess their comprehension, and adjust new information in light of past knowledge. The outcome is a student who is more proficient.

Although teacher explanation was preferable than providing no explanation at all, research has also shown that self-explanation is more successful. Stated differently, the first advantage of self-explain stems from the content, whereas the second benefit arises from the distinct method of producing an explanation. up order to fill up any comprehension gaps, students must be able to make connections between the material they have studied and their current understanding. In situations when individuals are prohibited from conducting independent research, the effectiveness of self-explanation is significantly reduced.

Teachers are advised to teach their pupils in this method because it is not thought of as a natural study habit. If this coaching is not provided, students may eventually find themselves concentrating just on repeating the procedures of a single problem, which will reduce their comprehension of the problem overall and prevent their abilities from being transferred. When there is a conceptual error in this self-explanation, students may pick up inaccurate information.

Because they believe they have learnt something and are unable to recognize the errors in their idea, this may have a greater impact on their education than their not comprehending a concept at all. Furthermore, the efficacy of this strategy may be limited to certain learning objectives or by the alternative teaching approach that it is contrasted with.

Additionally, by encouraging justifications for accurate information, this method is more likely to enhance learning. To ensure that the explanation prompts support the desired learning objectives, they must be properly crafted. Finally, compared to unguided studying, prompted self-explanation is more effective; nevertheless, other successful teaching strategies still need to be used.

Summarization

Since summarizing demands a thorough understanding of the subject matter, it is a very powerful tool for students. In order to reinforce comprehension of the key ideas, the strategy also calls for the learner to reread the content or some of it. It makes a distinction between the essential concepts that have to be covered in the summary and those that may be left out. Additionally, the student must rewrite ideas in their own terms. Because of this, it offers a great deal of flexibility in terms of condensation level based on the learner's objectives.

All of these activities, in general, improve learning. The most impactful amount of time spent reading a book, article, or subject is any number of hours. Additionally, considering the relative significance of imperfect information enhances analytical and critical thinking abilities. Rewriting the essay in one's own terms improves comprehension and recall as well. More precisely, because it forces students to simplify the content, summarizing any portion of the knowledge in fewer words improves learning as well. It eliminates less important facts and instances in order to concentrate on what is most important and to condense the content.

Making the results shorter than the original material is a necessary step in the summarization process. By doing this, one keeps the most significant or crucial notions, leaves out fewer crucial ideas, and condenses less crucial elements, or narratives. Any summary will differ according on how much condensation is used. This in turn is dependent upon the data at hand and the summary's intended purpose.

While some summaries condense the content to a tenth of the original text, others may only provide a third of it.

A lengthy original will have a more reduced summary. A student would not wish to, for instance, condense a 1000-page book into a 30 size (300 pages) since the work would be too taxing and 300 pages would be too much content to cover for one study session. Summaries are meant to be brief, easily comprehensible resources for emphasizing the most important points in a book, article, or other piece of information.

When summarizing, one must work closely with the available material or information. The learner needs to know why the summary exists. Is the summary a component of a learning tool, or is it intended to serve as a study guide or preserve important information for later use? Next, the essential concepts that should be highlighted in addition to the primary theme. At this stage, the student also decides which supporting information or examples to reduce or remove, as well as which inferior concepts may be left out.

One final piece of advice for high-performance summarizing is to skim book summaries or abstracts before beginning to read. In this case, the student may find that the review is sufficient. Secondly, by reading only the first phrase of each paragraph, one might employ summary shortcuts. This approach can occasionally provide a concise synopsis of the chapter or book being summarized. It is possible to discern between the significant and the insignificant when one keeps their feeling of progress in mind.

Underlining

This method highlights the information that is essential to the students' reading goals, helping them to arrange the material they have learned. Pupils are instructed to underline just the concepts and phrases that are essential to improving their understanding and proficiency of the material. This is a very adaptable tactic that may be applied with a variety of knowledge and abilities. This method may also be used to include technology-based material, like eBooks. This method of selective highlighting aids in getting students to focus more on the important details in a book.

    The instructor explains the technique to the class and goes over the goal of the exercise in the step-by-step method. After that, the process is shown to make sure the pupils know how to use the method.

    After that, students are provided with the time and resources to practice the technique and reinforce their good performance. They are watched over while they labor. Following the strategy's introduction, the instructor assigns the students to read the text and identify, underline, and highlight the main concepts and the details that support them. Only once the learner has read the paragraph or section through to the conclusion should they highlight it. Before highlighting, students should pause to consider what they have read and identify the key points.

    The only information highlighted is that which is necessary vocabulary. Following that, a summary paragraph is written using the data that has been highlighted. Students use this method to sort through the important and irrelevant material. When teaching this tactic to pupils, a teacher's sole restriction is their creativity. The student may also think about summarizing the important ideas in their own words, in a different set of notes, or in the margins.

This strategy's primary benefit is that it takes less time than taking notes and maintains context for individual information. The primary drawback is that it is only useful when applied judiciously to highlight key concepts and pertinent facts; underlining an entire page, including unimportant details, is ineffective. The second is that students who employ this method essentially focus their mental resources on classifying the information into categories based on importance. Students may find it easy to narrow their attention to emphasize specifics at the expense of developing a better comprehension of the whole picture. Students who choose this strategy also frequently make use of the highlighted passages in the book as the main focus of their study.

Keyword Mnemonic

One of the most important and beneficial techniques for using memory tricks to help learn and memorize material that is thought to be difficult to recall is this one. These details may be lists, the spelling of challenging words, or mathematical formulas. This method should be simple for teachers and students to understand and use.

In addition, it is inexpensive to apply and enjoyable. Furthermore, after mastering this method, students use it to stay organized and remind themselves of critical knowledge for the rest of their lives.

The method makes connections between a novel concept or term and well-known terms with similar sounds. By forming a mental image that correlates to this relationship, the learner can facilitate the storage and retrieval of more information as needed. As an illustration, suppose a teacher wishes to help pupils recall that Japan will host the 2022 Summer Olympics.

The ideal strategy is to give both terms a keyword phrase. Assuming that Japan is "Ja-a-Pan," "O-limp-x" is the Olympic key phrase. Aspiring pupils may see the millions of spectators at the Games chowing down on pan-fried food; this vivid mental image will help them recall the just acquired information. This would be the ideal method to use when a teacher is working with difficult new vocabulary terms. SUCCESS is another example that may be easily remembered by forming a mental image of "think-idea-try-do-do again-and-again-keep doing."

The primary use of the keyword technique is seen to be in the instruction of foreign languages. This tactic consists of an ongoing procedure that connects the foreign and local worlds like a key. A student who follows a methodical approach to learning a new language is given an indigenous word that has some elements of a foreign word. The next step in the process is to make the connection between the meaning of the native term and the foreign word's counterpart. This is accomplished by using verbal or visual imagery. The chosen term should preferably match the unknown word's sound or symbols. Secondly, the correlation between the target word and the keyword should be distinct in the sense that auditory cues like flavor, tone.

Memory retrieval is attributed to this technique. It helps pupils arrange the knowledge in relation to previously learned material that is already ingrained in their long-term memory. Finally, by giving pupils retrieval cues or aids, the technique helps them recover the information from long-term memory at a later time. It is best to apply the technique sparingly, though, as it can occasionally become laborious and worsen students' learning processes by creating confusion. Mnemonics can be a barrier to remembering knowledge if their correctness is not evaluated. Finally, they may give pupils the impression that they grasp concepts or have expertise in areas that they do not.

Imagery for Text

Using visual representations of text elements while reading or listening is the approach in question. Using this method will improve excellent academic achievement. These mental or visual representations help by enhancing how well the text integrates the information. The learner establishes a personal connection between the author's work and their experiences and past knowledge. Students practice conjuring up pictures in their minds when they read a passage or text. The learning method is the same for both individuals and groups. Because visualization is necessary to be able to form the mental images that help the learner comprehend what is happening in the tale, it becomes essential to understanding.

When students are having trouble understanding what they are reading, this is a great tactic to use. It helps to create situations or pictures that match the content. For instance, a student may find it difficult to comprehend a tale about a mountain, but if they envision it and pay attention to important features, they will be able to perceive it. When pupils use this strategy, learning becomes more relaxed for them.

When teaching pupils about imagery in text, they start reading and stop after a few texts that include descriptive content.

After that, they describe the mental images they had formed and quote specific passages from the book that had assisted in their mental imagery. This image may allude to the setting, the people in it, or the activities. The learner is modeling the type of mental images that one would like a youngster to have by doing this.

The discussion of how these images aid in understanding is the next stage. The reading then goes on before pausing once more. The newly produced photos are distributed. Through repetition of the words that helped the learner form the mental images and feelings, the student practices this ability.

The learner must read longer passages of material and carry out the sharing process as they get proficient with the approach. After being fully acquainted, the student may now confidently employ visuals in their mind to comprehend the text in a special way. The similar method may be used to help learners picture how to solve problems by starting with the finish in mind while learning arithmetic principles. The learner looks at the problem and illustrations of how to get to the right solution when working on arithmetic. They then consider the actions required to find the answer.

Re-reading

Most students read academic texts again in order to study. However, the majority of psychologists and educators have also criticized this approach. It is viewed as a very bad method of learning a subject. This is the preferred method for the majority of pupils. Rehashing information over and over again isn't a very good approach to acquire concepts or ideas, nor does it help form lasting memories. Students who only concentrate on reading a text again will not comprehend it any more than those who read it only once. Much knowledge should be gained from the first reading, but a sense of "I know this" undermines the second.

In essence, the learner is not selecting additional facts from the text or thoroughly processing the information. Rereading material may sometimes give the impression that one understands it all very well but, in reality, there may be multiple gaps in understanding. When utilizing this method, some useful advice is to read aloud before attempting a self-assessment with either prepared or made-up questions. Learning is strengthened when that knowledge is retrieved from memory.

In cases when retrieval presents difficulties, the self-assessment will provide a precise assessment of the knowledge gaps, indicating to the student where they need to focus their study efforts. This facilitates more efficient study techniques for pupils.

Students will comprehend more when they ask questions throughout the actual reading process. The learner will provide explanations in response to questions, which will improve and solidify comprehension. The student's memory is then sharpened as a result. Put differently, the approach need to allow for self-reflection in order to facilitate comprehension of the subject matter.

Relating the ideas or principles in the book to something the learner is already familiar with is another helpful rereading tactic. Or, to improve learning, make use of previous knowledge while referring to any new material. According to cognitive experts, rereading is very beneficial—but only if it also incorporates information retrieval. This phenomenon is known as the testing effect. However, it makes sense why the majority of pupils choose this method of rereading. Testing for comprehension is labor-intensive because it calls for an excessive amount of resilience. There is a widespread misconception that learning is easier when it is simple, yet research has repeatedly refuted this. More quizzes, examinations, or homework are the last thing students think about since they find them to be quite stressful.

Practice Testing

Studies show that the mention of exams, quizzes, and testing causes a great deal of anxiety in both teachers and students. On the other hand, students who take this mindset may be losing out on the advantages of one of the best ways to enhance learning. Research has demonstrated that practice exams enhance student performance and that taking them—as opposed to just rereading the content to be learned—can significantly increase learning. It is well known that students who report utilizing mock examinations as a study tool for exams do better.

In a similar vein, teachers who used these practice examinations reported that their students significantly improved on subsequent tests that included the material they had learned via daily inspections. Stated differently, pupils who assess themselves improve their long-term memory. Secondly, if a student is unable to accurately retrieve an answer on a quiz or exam, it indicates that they need to review the solution. By using this technique, teachers and students may decide for themselves what need more training and what doesn't. The majority of students utilize practice exams to assess their knowledge and weaknesses. Any type of practice exam will be helpful to a student.

The most crucial thing is that students should develop a culture of constant self-testing with feedback responses in their learning. This needs to become engrained in them until they can accurately recall every idea from memory.

They have a higher likelihood of understanding ideas and more complex subjects if they are persistent. By selecting the key concepts and periodically testing students at the start or close of each session, teachers may help to solidify this teaching strategy. After that, the teacher can quickly offer feedback by giving suitable responses. The most important material that will come up on the test should preferably be covered during the testing period that occurs during class hours. This guarantees that students will learn what their professors value most and also confirms.

Distributed Practice

With this study strategy, the student divides up the work they put into a particular subject over a number of shorter study periods. When this method is applied, meaningful learning occurs in sharp contrast to massed practice, which is defined by rote learning. Students that use scattered practice approaches in their schooling will usually outperform those who adhere to massed procedures.

This method is renowned for producing long-term retention with a reduced need for further mnemonic devices. The learner must strategically space out the learning units and provide time for quizzes. If a pupil wants to use this method, they must be very motivated and persistent. Establishing weekly study schedules at the start of each semester is a smart place to start. Set aside, say, an hour per day for each lesson. You should do this from Monday through Saturday.

The timetable might need to be adjusted once the semester starts because some classes can demand more than one study session each day.

The only person who can determine whether adjustments are necessary is the learner. The learner has to be able to adhere to the study plan in order for this strategy to work. Sometimes, nevertheless, a student could find it hard to anticipate what they would have to cope with a month from now. The creation of a learning timetable in such a high-uncertainty setting is thus unachievable. In such cases, dispersed practice may be largely replaced by obtaining study information from several sources utilizing diverse media.

When engaging in dispersed practice, a typical session might start with recalling context, which helps us retain what we've already learned. For this, flashcards might be a helpful tool.

Sometimes, in order to understand what we are reading, it is necessary for us to quickly review what we have already learned. The student then prepares two or three learning sets, each lasting 20 minutes and interspersed with brief breaks. Practice questions are then created as a recap of the material covered and are saved for discussion at the subsequent session.

When there are many sources available for a given topic, the student can practice switching between them. Instead of using only one source, the student might employ the dispersed practice strategy in these instances. The pupil moves on to another source after finishing the previous one. By doing this, the student becomes fully involved in the subject matter, ensuring long-term memory. As a result, the learner also feels less exhausted.

In conclusion, a wealth of empirical data establishes dispersed practice as one of the most successful approaches. The tactic is rather simple to comprehend and use. On the other hand, student learners might need additional support in the shape of motivation to use the method as well as some coaching in creating their study timetables. Distributed practice, on the other hand, will guarantee that many students grasp content they never imagined they could learn rapidly.

Interleaved Practice

This method combines dividing up the practice into different study periods and rearranging the study materials according to different subjects.

Over time, the same learning issue practice is dispersed. Given that both interleaved practice and distributed practice include spacing out one's practice across time, they are quite comparable. On the other hand, practicing different types of learning throughout time is explicitly referred to as an interleaved practice.

One instance would be algebra, where pupils are taught how to add and subtract real numbers. After that, they practice learning how to acquire real numbers and then work on a block of subtraction. The next chapter covers the concepts of real number multiplication and division, concentrating on the operations of multiplying, dividing, and so on. Here, the strategy is to practice a number of examples of one kind of arithmetic issue before moving on to the next.

Using the same example, interleaving entails handling a new problem from each of the several assigned categories after resolving one of each kind (addition, subtraction, multiplication, and division). In comparison to dispersed practice or practice exams, this strategy has not received as much attention. Interleaved practice, however, has been shown to considerably raise student success, particularly in this area of problem-solving.

Improved mastery of already acquired skills, quicker acquisition of new ones, and enhanced retention of newly learned material are further advantages of this strategy. Pupils undertaking technical learning skills practice benefit from utilizing a variety of examples from various categories. More so than training kids to practice with the same kind of models every time, this enhances their technical skills. Additionally, studying many concepts that are similar at the same time avoids confusion.

All things considered, implementing this strategy in the educational process has several advantages.

3

CHAPTER 3: IMPORTANT STUDY TACTICS

A student's time is devoted to studying for several hours.
   A well-adjusted student has to schedule social activities in addition to their studies in order to have a balanced existence.

CHAPTER 3: IMPORTANT STUDY TACTICS

Studies are also likely to struggle and fall short of the high standards set in their absence. Thus, if motivated students want to succeed, they need to create and implement efficient study strategies. In this chapter, strategies that are most likely to have a major influence on learners' academic performance will be discussed.

Create a Study Schedule You Can Stick To

There are several ideas or topics in characterisation that students must grasp or at least demonstrate competency with. But because time is a limited resource, most students occasionally find it difficult to study for every topic. Making a study schedule is one method to make sure your studies are balanced. That said, it is easier said than done.

In addition to learning, there are obligations to friends and family that must be balanced. It suggests that in order to help learners organize both their lives and their academics, we must embrace a creative tool.

The pupils' assessment of their present time management practices is the first stage. It allows one to determine what activities a student might be able to forgo in order to ensure productivity and where learning can be made more effective. To begin with, it is crucial to ascertain how many hours a student spends on their academics, extracurricular activities, leisure, and other non-academic pursuits each week.

The following stage is to consider one's work ethics so that the timetable may be planned. The curriculum need to outline the student's expected work style. If there will be a lot of time spent on breaks or other errands, the plan should account for that. The learner must begin cognitively connecting certain acts, such opening a textbook or sitting down at a desk, with being in a study mindset after a habit has been formed. A concise and comprehensive list of all the subjects that need to be studied is created, along with the courses. The student is responsible for determining what is needed for each class session.

Setting priorities for the previously created list is the next stage. Students can determine which courses require the most time by ranking each class according to priority. When completing this, the student should consider the level of difficulty of the question or test, the quantity of reading needed, and the quantity of review needed for each item on the list. The total amount of time allotted to study throughout a week. The student might then proceed to designate the blocks to certain subjects. The student must make sure that time is set up for other activities involving family and friends in addition to the time allotted for each task. A student cannot be successful in their academics until they develop.

Establish a Study Approach That Suit You

A student must determine the optimal learning strategy for them in order to be productive and successful in their academics. In order to get optimal essay marks and test scores, students must identify and choose a learning style that maximizes productivity. Even if this is learned by trial and error, the advice provided should offer a student some important considerations to make while choosing the most effective strategy.

   The first approach that is really beneficial is taking notes, which is a traditional learning strategy. Copying passages from books, summarizing ideas on notecards, dedicating a page to each topic, or making unending reams of notes and filing them are all examples of note-taking techniques. The primary issue with taking notes is that it is too simple to repeat what a teacher says without paying attention to the content. If a student attempts this strategy and then discovers that they are unable to respond to test questions on a certain reviewed topic, this may indicate that they have not yet discovered their preferred learning style.

Learning by doing, or having students try things out in real life, is one of the most successful learning approaches. A scientific experiment to ascertain the mechanism of a chemical reaction would be one example. A literature student could also try out for a role in a musical or play that the class is studying. For a deeper understanding of important historical events, history students might pay a visit to the locations of notable historical landmarks. Engaging in practical experiences provides the brain with a tangible memory boost, which facilitates the retrieval of information around test time.

Learners that have a strong desire to succeed may choose to focus more on examinations and practice exams. Students that thrive on difficulties are the ones targeted for the mocks and evaluations. These ongoing assessments may be given by teachers or other participants in the research group.

Visual learners will benefit from the visual method of learning since they have a tendency toward visual memory. Methods like making mind maps for every subject taught are part of the visual memory. With arrows pointing to the facts that need to be ascertained, the topic name is in the center. The indications help students visualize their memories and remember the order of data on a certain note sheet, which makes them an effective memory aid during exams.

For certain people, learning in a group—also known as social learning—works best. This strategy aids in overcoming emotions of loneliness. Furthermore, it is hegemonic in that it compels students to openly challenge and defend their beliefs.

Students who prefer to solve issues over receiving answers

can consider adopting a learning approach that emphasizes deduction. Students with a preference for the sciences are best suited for this type of instruction.

Lastly, visual learning, often known as imagery, facilitates knowledge absorption for certain kids. For people who find it difficult to study subjects from books, visual learning is an appropriate approach. It's ideal for learning literature as well. Students will come to learn that they may retain or comprehend material better if they listen to an audio version of the book.

Designate a Study Area

A student may study more productively and raise their marks considerably in a space that is efficient, pleasant, and well-organized.

Students can improve their study area with the help of the following advice.

The student has to choose a space that they will use just for learning. When you choose a location, it facilitates the brain's instinctive shift into work mode when entering that space. The ideal location for the place would be away from distractions, with a desk and a chair that are comfortable enough to promote proper posture. The student should use a curtain to separate their workplace from other distractions in their room if the study area is in a garage or bedroom.

The desk for studying must be organized. The ideal method is to store files inside the cabinets in folders and books in book holders. It will be helpful to put announcements, study aids, notes, and reminders on a bulletin board. Last but not least, having and carrying a calendar is a necessary tool for remembering deadlines for assignments, tests, extracurricular activities, and other significant events. There should be no clutter on the desk. A busy environment, as they say, contributes to a cluttered mind. The workspace need to be orderly. It's also crucial to have a file system to recycle outdated examinations and assignments and save pertinent materials.

Students are more productive and focused when there is adequate illumination, therefore their study desk should be next to a window.

Another helpful technique is to utilize aromas and colors to create an energized ambiance. Light blue is a relaxing hue that will increase productivity.

Fragrances also have an impact on mood. The allocated study area should be fragrant before starting to study in order to foster an encouraging and productive atmosphere. Distractions of any kind should be avoided during studying. Switch off your game consoles and television. If background noise is required, gentle classical music is recommended. Students should not be using social media sites like Facebook, Twitter, Wattsup, and others that seriously distract them. It will take a lot of resolve to avoid their attempts at productivity-eroding fun.

Finally, when the body is properly nourished, learning becomes more fun. It is very recommended that you eat a lot of fresh vegetables, protein bars, or fruits as a snack before starting your study job. During study periods, a jug of water can also be kept nearby. A student will stay focused and improve as a learner if they take the time to set up the ideal study space.

Note Taking-Outline and Re-write Your Notes

One of the things that helps a student succeed is taking notes.

Recalling knowledge that would otherwise be forgotten is aided by this exercise.

But as simple as it may seem, taking notes properly involves more than just recording what the lecturer says. An easy-to-remember summary of key topics is a necessary component of effective note-taking. It must be written in the student's preferred manner.

This approach to taking notes will help the student examine key ideas or concepts and help them prepare for a lecture. In addition to actively engaging in class, the student will need to be sharp and attentive in order to maintain attention. Overall, taking notes effectively can help students improve their abilities and reduce stress when exam time approaches.

This approach to taking notes will help the student examine key ideas or concepts and help them prepare for a lecture. In addition to actively engaging in class, the student will need to be sharp and attentive in order to maintain attention. Overall, taking notes effectively can help students improve their abilities and reduce stress when exam time approaches.

Furthermore, using this strategy, students may rapidly determine where to insert models, basic concepts, examples, pros, disadvantages, and authors for various knowledge levels by creating their own keys.

Symbols or colored text can also be used to distinguish between different levels.

Additionally, gaps are allowed between topics so that students can return and take more notes. Using the approach to outline the major ideas to be covered and then add indentations to record supporting points and other information may also be helpful when preparing an essay plan.

The outline approach is seen to be the most effective and current for students. The method saves a lot of time that can be used for additional reviewing and editing by assisting the learner in structuring their notes. The approach asks the learner to utilize bullet points to organize their notes, with each point indicating a separate topic or subtopic. To put it another way, the records may be arranged using text indentation to separate the major points from the details in hierarchies of points. Notes arranged as follows: "the main topic>subtopic>key concept>supporting details" would be a typical example.

Because the strategy rationally accentuates important lecture ideas, students enjoy it.

Following the lecture, the student reviews their notes to

make sure they understand them better and, if needed, rapidly rewrites what they missed. A learner can therefore quickly understand the connections between various themes and subtopics. Because of its simplicity of use, students are able to concentrate better and spend less time editing and reviewing afterward. Without a doubt, it works better than taking paragraph-style notes. It is also simple to convert the presented information into study questions. The approach provides a student's notes with an appropriate and tidy framework in terms of organizing.

Nevertheless, it has been determined that the approach is inappropriate for science-related courses using formulas, graphs, and charts. In lectures without a set format, it is not a good idea to take notes using this method. It could also take some time for a pupil to become accustomed to the procedure. But, it becomes rapid and natural if a learner grasps which knowledge is essential at each stage.

Use of Memory Games

Recent research has cast doubt on widely held beliefs about how learning occurs and supported the idea that retrieving knowledge is essential for long-term, lasting learning. Each time, a student's memory is recovered, making it easier for them to access in the future. Retrieving all that knowledge, however, is a completely different story. A learner can improve their short- and long-term memory with the use of a number of strategies and memory games.

The student must either use or lose their memory. A learner's ability to retain and recall knowledge improves with increased brain exercise. The most effective brainteasers are those that push learners outside of their comfort zone to employ and create new neural pathways.

Whatever a pupil choose to do to improve their memory has to be outside of their comfort zone and unfamiliar. Continued learning and skill development are necessary for brain strengthening in students. The same brain-boosting exercises have to be difficult enough to demand a learner's whole focus. It must be something that normally takes a lot of mental work, like learning to play a new instrument in music. One must also be able to advance through the activity as their abilities grow. Their capacity is always being pushed by their special powers. A formerly challenging level that begins to feel comfortable should be replaced with the next higher degree of performance. Finally, mental exercises ought to be ones that reinforce the process of learning through incentives. It ought to be fulfilling as well as pleasurable.

Jigsaw puzzles are one type of memory game that might improve cognitive abilities. They are thought to be a great instrument for stimulating short-term memory. Through juggling, the brain puts together visual representations by organizing a range of colors and forms. The more parts in this jigsaw, the more effort the brain must put in. It has been demonstrated that clicking on the pieces improves concentration.

For years, newspapers have also been fond of Sudoku, a numbers game. Playing this game requires a student to use their memory skills a lot. mentally practicing placement in nine-space grids and mentally running through a series of numbers. It should be noted that Sudoku is thought to be most beneficial in the early stages, when the brain is still becoming used to sorting numbers. It might be time to tackle a different task later on, if it begins to feel more natural for the student.

For many years, crossword puzzles have been a useful mental workout.

There is a link between those who become addicted to this mental activity and the delayed onset of dementia. It undoubtedly improves brain function and memory.

In order to keep their minds active, students who select this activity to improve their memory might also try other word games.

Another stimulating game that students can play to improve their cognitive abilities is chess. Skilled participants acquire the ability to commit tactics to their long-term memory; the activity changes to merely remembering information for the extended duration. In order to assess the chessboard and plan their moves, less experienced players rely more on their short memories.

Practice by Yourself or With Friends

Good practice makes perfect when it comes to academic study. In theory, exams and tests are one means of evaluating comprehension and knowledge. However, obtaining a decent education is the primary goal of learning.

However, examinations are also quite important, and many educational institutions prepare their pupils to pass tests. A pupil needs to practice a lot, just like they would in chess or football. Teachers will probably advise their students to use past exam papers to self-assess. One of the strongest strategies for raising academic achievement is the one that entails practicing under time constraints. Research from several sources demonstrates that it is beneficial for students in preschool, graduate school, and professional training. They are putting themselves to the test since the Students try to retrieve knowledge from their memory. It is not often that we are just going over our notes or reading academic texts again.

It is more efficient to retrieve than to just restudy. In addition to the real subject to study, practice examinations aid in understanding the scope, complexity, and type of questions to be expected. If there isn't a practice exam accessible, students can create one for themselves and their peers. The most fruitful group studies are those that are small and comprise students in the same class who have comparable academic backgrounds. The strategy will be different from groups as well. Some people would rather go through the chapters together and test each other as they go. Others will decide to Verify the materials and verify the class notes to make sure they have not overlooked any important ideas or concepts.

There are other ways to prepare for tests, such as using

flashcards, going over online tests again, and responding to pre-made questions at the conclusion of each chapter. The best results from these tests come from avoiding true-false or multiple-choice questions. The student must give them a free call. It's also not a good idea to test yourself right away after studying. It is obvious that students tend to greatly overestimate their knowledge of a subject or body of material when they are just starting to study it.

It might be wiser to obtain some sleep in between study sessions. Memory consolidation is believed to happen as you sleep, thus a student is more likely to retain information for a longer period of time than if they study for the same length of time without taking a nap. Additionally, it's likely that the learner will learn the content more quickly when they return to study it after taking a nap. Overall, taking practice exams by yourself or with friends should not be interpreted as an evaluation but rather as a means of determining where the individual's knowledge gaps are and how best to direct their efforts.

Learn How to Deal With Difficult Material

The capacity to take in demanding or complex academic material is a crucial talent that shows excellent performance. It is common for students to encounter reading content that appears to be beyond their comprehension, whether it be a few pages, a journal article, or a whole book; it can easily cause them to feel overwhelmed. The kinds of abilities that an employer will compensate you for in that ideal job after graduation are the ones that come from learning to read and comprehend difficult study materials.

Reading and processing difficult material requires focus or just breaking the task down into manageable pieces. The student must realize that comprehension of required texts that are not discussed in class is their responsibility. By acknowledging that learning is a responsibility the content, they will make an effort to utilize the study resources effectively, leading to a greater amount of learning. Regrettably, a lot of instructors have to explain difficult readings to their pupils since they are aware of how poorly they read. Consequently, the pupils continue to be bad readers since they are aware that the professor will still read the materials. Thus, we are left with a regrettable cyclical cycle.

Nonetheless, a focused and committed learner would do well to begin by stating why they are reading the difficult material. Is the student learning to extract specifics, or is he or she just skimming the surface to obtain the gist? A committed reader understands that not all books are created equal and that some sections, paragraphs, or chapters will be more challenging than others. First, the student should select a chapter or paragraph that begins with a decent amount of material. They scan the section for subjects, subtopics, headings, and subheadings to grasp the basic idea once they have a firm understanding of how the content is organized. A summary should be included at the end of each chapter as it will assist the learner with reviews. While you're at it, go ahead and read what you comprehend to get a sense of how complex the subject is. Then, see whether there are any questions or exam exercises after that. What the student does not understand is noted for future review.

The pupil reads, and as he or she should get into the habit of taking short breaks from the text to pose thought-provoking questions to herself that are specifically related to the book. Next, they answer using their own words.

The goal of this exercise should be to comprehend the content, not simply memorize it. Attempts should be made to establish linkages and correlations during that process. Look up any complex words in the dictionary that are crucial to comprehending the material. They should have two dictionaries handy while they read: one for important terms they don't understand and another that is more focused on the book's content. The pupil should make an effort to finish reading without giving up. The more a student learns, the more obvious the material will become. Finally, go over the full a chapter or paragraph to determine what has been remembered. It is crucial that they connect topics in order to organize their notes as a single review. It is advised to apply whatever method is most effective. To illustrate and link ideas, tools such as graphics, photos, and colors can be used. It's time to put the reading away and try to restudy it the next day if the student still does not understand it at this point. Repeat as needed. Repeating enables distributed reading, in which the information is processed by the brain even when the reader is asleep. The learner is urged to speak with their instructor, counselor, or reading specialist if the study's topic continues to be difficult.

4

CHAPTER 4: TEN EFFECTIVE TIPS AND HACKS TO SAVE YOUR TIME AND LEARN FASTER

As they say, time is of the essence. The proverb is especially applicable to time-pressed college students who are expected to balance their social lives, part-time jobs, and classes and homework.

They excel at their coursework. Some, on the other hand, manage to get decent results while maintaining an active social life and spending little time studying. The main factor behind this discrepancy is the efficiency—or inefficiency—of time management.

This chapter will go over ten strategies that have been tested and shown to help students study more quickly and efficiently while saving time.

While some of them may appear unusual, they actually function.

Go to the Source, Find a Practical Approach From Teachers

It's not always the case that better student-teacher connections translate into higher performance. Nonetheless, history shows that pupils who have a close-knit support system with their teachers

indeed outperform those who are under stress in terms of their accomplishments.

Expertise in the subject matter is a crucial component of good teaching. Proficiency in an instructor's field has a significant impact on pupils' ability to learn more rapidly. Teachers could benefit from targeted support to help them gain a deeper grasp of specific areas where their expertise is lacking. This could help them improve their practical guidance skills and approach to teaching.

We can use the case of a student who, by communicating with her on a regular basis and receiving personalized attention from her, feels safe and connected to her instructor. scholarly advice on occasion. That student is probably going to perform better academically, demonstrate greater enthusiasm in her studies, and have greater faith in her teacher. Additionally, the learner is more likely to find learning more approachable and to pick up concepts more quickly as a result. A positive, favorable interaction between the instructor and the students is beneficial to the learning process and increases the students' desire to learn.

The first action that can establish a solid basis for facilitating faster and more accessible learning is for the instructor to maintain a daily teaching log or journal. The left side of the teaching notebook will be used for comments and reflection, while the right side will have the instructor's lesson plan. Queries questions to ask oneself include "What went well in today's class? Where did the kids appear to be struggling?

In the upcoming session, which areas might require further clarification? What should I alter the next time I instruct on this subject?" In the long run, this type of self-reflection facilitates student learning by continuously informing the instructor's instruction.

Teachers also need to know that learning is introduced gradually when pupils are given the time to practice new abilities. Students realize that they may learn a subject more quickly and easily as time goes on. Learning progress made by students continues to be the most important metric used to evaluate instructors' effectiveness. Therefore, it should be obvious that a hands-on approach that helps pupils learn quickly by efficient evaluation and questioning techniques.

Teachers' beliefs are also essential in helping children learn at an accelerated rate. Their goals and actions in the classroom have an impact on the development of their students. How well a teacher understands chemistry and what it takes to master it has an impact on the way their students learn.

It is important to understand that the trainer-student dynamic influences the classroom environment, which in turn impacts the way in which students learn. The concept establishes a learning atmosphere in the classroom where students are held to higher standards and are encouraged to put in more effort than talent. It makes learning easier by allowing behind pupils to put in more effort to master the material establishing connections and a Student learning has improved as a result of teachers' professional conduct, which includes parent conversations.

Motivation and involvement are greatly influenced by frequent communication between the teacher and the student, both within and outside of the classroom. Instructor concerns assist pupils in overcoming obstacles and concentrating on their academics. Getting to know certain teachers well also helps students focus more intently on their studies and inspires them to consider their goals and ideals. The teacher holds after-class review sessions, introduces activities that bring students to the teacher's office for consultation, shares previous experiences with the class, attends and supports student-led activities, and uses email to inspire and occasionally relay information to the students.

Second, in order to guarantee collaboration rather than isolation among pupils, a practical instructor must also promote cooperation among them. and rivalry between students. Students' comprehension is deepened when they respond to each other's thoughts and share their own. In addition to using case studies and group discussions in the classroom, the teacher can encourage students to study for tests or exams together. They can also be asked to exchange background information and academic interests with one another. Finally, teachers may assign pupils to have discussions about important ideas with classmates whose perspectives and worldviews are different from their own.

In order to promote engaged and hands-on learning, the teacher needs to recognize that education is not a spectator sport. It is necessary to extend an invitation to the student to discuss, write, and connect what they are learning to real-world applications. Teachers carry out this task efficiently. by mandating that students present in front of their peers, promoting the utilization of study abroad and internship opportunities.

Additionally, it's critical to employ technology to support

active learning, encourage the reading of scholarly publications, and ask students to submit specific, real-world scenarios for analysis.

Giving pupils timely performance feedback is another useful strategy. For learners to gain from the study, appropriate feedback is necessary. Students require many opportunities in the classroom to not only perform but also receive feedback on how to go better. As their studies come to a conclusion, they should also have time to think on the new concepts, the areas in which they still need improvement, and the most effective way for them to evaluate themselves. In order to accomplish this, the teacher must arrange brief discussions about the pupils' progress during the meetings. Exam results should be returned immediately. Students should also receive written feedback on the merits and shortcomings of their tests and papers, as well as feedback on their work early in the term. Furthermore, the teacher must be open and honest about how performance level and expectations relate to grades.

High expectations must be communicated in order for instruction to be effective, for both the well-prepared and the bright and driven students. When you anticipate that pupils will perform very well High expectations from instructors only lead to a self-fulfilling prophecy when it comes to student performance. At the start of the course, the instructor should make sure that all expectations are communicated in both written and spoken form. In addition, the teacher must establish the study rules and publish pupil contributions on a course webpage. Students can edit their work and receive motivation to succeed at better levels thanks to the publications.

An teacher must acknowledge that there are multiple pathways to education in order to make sure learning is simpler for students. Some students excel in practical learning but struggle in theoretical. Every student needs to be given the chance to showcase their skills and be given the freedom to learn in a way that suits them personally. If not, they will be forced to learn in ways that are incompatible with who they are. To reach students from a wide range of backgrounds, the instructor must use a variety of instructional strategies. One of the educational tasks is having students participate in various assignment formats, such as written and spoken as many learning methods as possible, figuring out each student's learning preferences and history at the start of the semester, and giving them more material if they don't have the necessary prior knowledge or abilities.

How to Prepare for Your Studies

A student must efficiently manage their time in order to fit their education in around any other obligations. The learner must think about how his or her education will be organized and fit into their schedule. Will it possible to set out particular times and days of the week for studying, or is it possible to be more flexible? The student must consider their own study habits (e.g., being a night owl or an early riser) and what works best for them while making this decision (smaller, more frequent study sessions vs longer, more focused ones).

To get ready for study, it's a fantastic idea to plan your journal.

Here, lessons are chosen, important dates are noted, and study time is scheduled as soon as feasible. If a student is not used to this, they should get used to it because they will have a lot on their plate and it will be difficult to study effectively if they are unable to meet deadlines. Here, the key is to establish and adhere to a plan.

Students will also benefit from time blocks that allow for extensive class periods or brief daily windows for checking message boards. These arrangements will help them get ready for their studies. Timetables that are being developed will require continuous reviews to ensure their accuracy and usefulness. Additionally, a little ingenuity will enable the learner to set aside time in short bursts for concentrated work. The assessment might take place during commutes, around lunch, or early in the morning. when study preparation is focused on the dawn hours.

A quality study space is an essential supplement to a well-prepared study regimen.

The place should have all necessary study materials, be well-lit, accessible when needed, and free from interruptions or distractions.

It's also critical that students remember to look after their physical needs. Maintaining physical health entails eating a balanced diet, obtaining enough sleep, and engaging in regular exercise. Diet and sleep are especially crucial for preserving one's physical and mental health.

Organizing Studying Materials

The fundamental guideline is to make every effort to keep course materials distinct from one another so that they are simple to find. The following are some recommendations on how students should arrange their lecture notes and other study resources.

Making sure to take the appropriate notes is the first step. Selecting the appropriate notes entails writing down information that the instructor says repeatedly.

Understanding the material or course will require paying attention to everything the teacher says again. Simply summarize the lecture or discussion's major points, and note any instances or hypotheticals—especially in the sciences or math.

The learner has the option to use a loose-leaf notepad with dividers to store study materials. Everything you need is right here. Classes can remain combined. All loose materials are gathered and placed next to related paperwork. Inserts made from photocopies can be included in the main report. If you fold them together, this method of organizing can be messy and somewhat unwieldy. Additionally, some study materials may come unfastened. Another option are folders with two pockets that can accommodate lecture notes and blank paper for future note-taking. The folder can be used to store additional teaching resources like handouts, completed assignments, and papers that have been returned. On the other hand, terrible things happen if you drop a folder, like on a windy day, and the essays tumble out. A briefcase is the greatest place to store binders.

Additionally, some folders are somewhat delicate and might break even before the semester is out. Lecture notes can be permanently bound in spiral notebooks. All records are promptly filed away for future reference at the end of the semester.

When taking electronic study notes through document creation or audio recording, the learner will have to handle digital data. Different approaches are used to handle digital data, such as making a distinct digital folder for every topic area. The paper can be different for each small topic and placed in the relevant directories; the files and folder names should make sense. Last but not least, page numbers and document labels ought to be included in the header or footer.

Maintaining a record of handouts and syllabi will also be extremely important for self-organization. They provide details the student will need to know about the course, the goal of the class, and homework assignments. In addition, these materials will include information about the kinds of essays and topics the students will need to know, which will help them decide what kind of notes to take in class.

Study Habits Inventory

The purpose of this inventory is to learn more about a student's potential use of different learning skills. You list a number of abilities for the rating, including test preparation, note-taking, focus, and comprehension.

It is thought that focused attention is a reliable indicator of productive study habits.

While some students need some time to get started, they can focus for extended periods of time, others cannot focus for very long. Others have absolutely no trouble focusing. While some people read solely when they feel like it, others need stimulation, so they'll drink tea or coffee to help them concentrate.

Understanding depends on a few certain student behaviors. For instance, a pupil can attempt to connect the information acquired in one subject with what was previously studied in another to assimilate fresh information. In an attempt to set a study style for a specific subject, others could attempt to catch up on what the teacher is covering.

The activity becomes a crucial part of study habits for students who have to study a variety of subjects and develop different levels of perception. For instance, some students set deadlines for finishing particular assignments, whereas others follow strict schedules and study a variety of disciplines.

Study sets are closely related to the aforementioned. The physical and situational features that a student adopts for study might be defined as the study settings. While some people read best at night, others find that unwinding on a couch helps them learn more. When other pupils attempt the same method, they eventually nod off. It is important to recognize that study habits are more general in nature than they are specific.

Eliminating Excuses

Excuses are a common tactic used by students to try and justify their behavior with regard to their performance, their efforts in particular classes, and the academic assignments they are unable to complete. Nonetheless, the primary cause of their inability to meet their academic objectives is their own excuses. Therefore, giving up on generating excuses in advance is one of the best habits a student can develop. Give up justifying their mistakes or a student's tardiness and begin making the essential preparations for a successful academic career.

The learner needs to start accepting responsibility as the first step in breaking this behavior. The student must accept personal accountability for their behavior and any resulting repercussions. Should they be incapable of doing so, then it becomes unfeasible for them to make any significant academic progress.

Students who break down their long-term academic goals into smaller, more manageable ones may also develop the habit of working toward those shorter ones.

They gain the motivation to move on to the next task once they reach a minor one.

Students just need to be aware of their weaknesses in those areas or courses; they don't need to concentrate on them. Rather, they ought to concentrate on the advantages that other pupils might not possess. To fill up the gaps in poor subjects, they can also think about speaking with professors or other coworkers.

Eliminating the possibility or habit of making excuses can also be accomplished by learning from prior failures. Through learning what not to do, mistakes aid in a student's growth. They are also capable of conducting a critical analysis to determine what went wrong and how to go differently, for example, in the upcoming semester or exam. Almost every mistake is a teaching moment.

A student must have a clear understanding of their academic goals before attempting to break this bad behavior. Excuses will only hinder the achievement of that goal and could cause one to spin in circles for years at a time with no forward motion.

Hints for Getting Organized

The main factor that makes students need to tidy their belongings is that it lowers their stress levels. Students are more likely to feel better and do better in class when they are less anxious. They've got more time to participate in different activities and are generally more enjoyable to be around. The kid will be able to lead a more productive life at school if they are organized in these crucial areas. The first piece of advice for organizing is to keep a calendar. Having to remember appointments, classes, due dates, and exam schedules is greatly relieved by them. Everything is arranged in a practical visual style. When utilizing an electronic calendar, one can internalized prompts.

A student must keep track of activities that need to be completed in addition to events, which are things that happen on a given day or time and call for physical presence. Another relevant tool that will elevate the situation is the task manager/to-do list, which serves as a reminder to students of tasks they have to complete. Usually, there is no requirement for the student to be at a specific location or to adhere to any form of appointment.

Another useful advice for a student to get organized is to take the appropriate notes.

The suggested approach is a digital platform that lets students make a "Notebook" for each class. When reviewing content, this method makes it much easier for the learner to do so.

Aside from taking notes, students can improve their organization skills by organizing all of their course materials into a digital system or a physical three-ring binder.

The course materials include of PowerPoint presentations, handouts, homework, and a syllabus.

Another strategy to be organized is to get enough sleep. Most days of the week, the student should be operating at full capacity, feeling rejuvenated and more capable of thinking clearly the following day.

Lastly, getting better organized will require the student to have weekly

productivity reviews to maintain their entire organizational system. Comparing what was in the attainment plan to the actual achievement is the task of the productivity reviews. These gaps were found are then incorporated into strategies. A student looks at the reasons behind what they haven't yet completed. The next few days or weeks can then see modifications based on this. The student becomes more adept at setting reasonable goals and adhering to a timetable as they develop this habit.

Focus on Time Management and Organization

We consider a pupil to be proficient in time management when he can set aside, divide, and distribute time. Finding strategies for energizing the mind and generating ideas is essential when working for extended periods of time. The following advice demonstrates many methods that a student might use to keep his mind engaged and fresh while studying. Before starting a study session, the student should confirm that they can complete the assignment in the allotted time. If you can divide a study assignment with a lot of information and complexity into smaller manageable assignments, it would be great. Splitting assists the students in increasing their self-assurance and desire as they work toward the more manageable objectives.

Adding diversity to one's study tasks is another tactic to prevent doing the the same thing for a considerable amount of hours. If not, the brain will quickly become exhausted and stop functioning. Prolonged study sessions must to be divided into shorter ones and routinely evaluated in light of the predetermined goals. At the conclusion of each chapter or two, the student should take full use of the natural breaks.

It's also a good idea to actively work toward removing barriers to efficient time management. These obstacles include, but are not limited to, difficulty focusing, a lack of drive, and a noisy study space.

The goal is to tackle the less interesting chores first, trying to ignore them, before moving on to more interesting activity.

To put it briefly, time management is a personal path that students must discover for themselves of keeping an eye on and organizing activities that work for them. You can use the records in situations when written lists are preferred. Plans and diagrams should be utilized in their place if working from them is preferable. Using a weekly planner to set clear goals for the days or weeks ahead, a term planner to measure productivity, and clarity in the work at hand are all ways to continuously reflect on one's approach to planning.

The process of organizing and exerting control over the amount of time spent on particular tasks is known as time management. It entails balancing obligations, social life, family, hobbies, and academics.

Whether they are aware of it or not, students are constantly choosing how to manage their time. They could choose When should I go to the gym, sleep, attend to class, study, or visit the library? Furthermore, how you manage your time is influenced by these choices. Students can follow these guidelines for efficient time management.

It is recommended that students have a minimum of seven to eight hours of sleep every night. The student needs to set aside at least twenty hours per week for their studies. There should be four or more distinct study activities per week. Plan to spend a maximum of 10 hours a day on schoolwork, with a maximum of five hours per subject.

Make time for breaks and occasionally schedule a day off from school. Remember that having a full schedule is depressing and ineffective.

The student should create a program that fits the rhythm of their social life and academics in order to help them stay to the timetable. They ought to be adaptable and able to change with the times. The student can isolate oneself and stay away from phones, emails, and texts in order to work effectively. The ability to say no is also essential to following time management guidelines. Students may have a lot of demands on their time, so they must be sure that their firmly planned schedule does not get thrown off by optional engagements.

Minimize Distractions

Most students have a tendency to underestimate the degree to which their surroundings distract them. Their capacity to focus while studying may be harmed by these distractions.

The following advice outlines how taking into account one's surroundings can help one get the most out of their study. First, make sure you turn off the internet. Google, Facebook, YouTube, and other websites are typically reachable via a computer by only touching the screen or hitting a button on the keyboard, or by using a mouse and keypad. Before beginning to study, it is advised that students turn off their device's internet connection. It's possible for a student to think they have self-control and neglect to check the social media pages for changes. When conducting research, the internet may be a very helpful resource for obtaining information. But it can also be a source of distraction. Because of the frequent distractions, using the internet might cause students to take an excessive amount of time to complete tasks.

The phone ought to be turned off and placed far away— possibly on the opposite side of the room. From now on, the student won't have to worry about being distracted by calls or texts while studying. You can handle the calls and notes that need to be answered right away later when you're taking a break. Disruptions of any kind should be avoided at all costs whilst studying.

The finest recommendation is to before you begin studying session, you must be deliberate in your efforts and ask that nobody, not even those in your immediate vicinity, interrupt you in any manner. Your request is more likely to be respected by others.

For a student who is dedicated to academic performance, sleep is extremely important. Sleep has an impact on brain function, memory, and focus. Students who don't get enough sleep do not position themselves to succeed academically. Distraction is an inevitable result of sleep loss. Having a nightly schedule is beneficial.

Likewise, abstaining from caffeine after 4 p.m. It can also be quite beneficial to set an alarm clock to remind you when to go to bed so that you have a regular sleeping schedule. The brain's ability to recognize a sleeping pattern also aids in the brain's normal operation.

Focus on Note-Taking Skills

Learning how to take notes helps students retain information, acquire useful learning abilities, and comprehend a subject better.

By making connections between various topics, paying attention to what the teacher is saying, and taking better study notes throughout class, one can enhance their memory and understanding of the content being covered. These notes also serve as excellent review material. Taking notes efficiently is one of the secrets to academic success. By taking precise and legible notes, students can review material that was unclear during the lecture, reinforce what they learned, and remember important details. They can also focus on particular subjects that are most important. The student can compare his to make sure they're accurate and comprehensive notes with those of other pupils.

Better notes are taken when preparation is done correctly. Preparation involves going over the recorded lectures from prior lectures and finishing the specified reading before class. It's a good idea to leave gaps in your notes so that additional information can be added later. This is particularly true when teachers cover a variety of subjects in a single lesson due to a lack of a coherent topic flow.

Using abbreviations when taking notes might assist cut down on the amount of time needed to compose a particular report or response. The first time you use the abbreviations in a written piece, it's best to clarify what they mean when you choose to utilize them. The students can design their own acronyms. For information, the learner can use tables or charts rather than paragraphs. Compared to paragraphs, tables and graphs help organize facts into a structured whole that is easier to recall.

Datting and recording course codes on all handouts are two other strategies to improve note-taking abilities, particularly when using loose papers or printed copies of materials. All of your pages need to have numbers on them. In order to use the examples and pictures to help you recall the information later, you must also title each portion of the brief notes. Make sure to accurately record all of the references, dates, proper names, and statistics before learning to compose it in your own words.

Student's Personal Shorthand System: To be able to You can design your own symbols or acronyms to help others understand your notes. The time it takes to create notes can be greatly decreased by using abbreviations. You may find yourself running out of time to write and explain everything if you take all of your notes by hand.

as it's not usually a good idea, there are situations in the classroom where writing as you listen becomes necessary. To help you understand the subject, you can write into longhand notes during your revision period once you have the shorthand notes.

Recognize issues with taking text notes.-Taking notes can seem easy at first, but errors can creep in very quickly. When taking notes during a lecture, seminar, or study session, any mistakes could cause a student's notes to become completely useless. The following advice can help you recognize these issues. If the student is having trouble drawing comparisons between her notes and those of her colleague, they should attempt dating all of their lecture notes and making sure to write the topic in the upper-right corner of each page. One way to address the issue of pages in a student's study notes that are completely covered with writing from top to bottom and side to side is to try skipping a few lines for each new topic. As an alternative, try indenting and numbering the details under a single topic when writing just one item per line and providing multiple details for a specific topic. Does the pupil discover it challenging to determine which things are crucial?

As a result, the student will be able to pay closer attention and identify situations in which the instructor restates the concept in a new way, reads aloud from her notes to ensure accuracy, or spells out a name or team when reviewing material from an earlier lecture. All of these need to indicate to the pupil how important the material being taught is. When taking notes, students should try to use acronyms if they notice that the lecturer has moved on to points 2, 3, and 4 while they are still attempting to write down position 1. In addition, they can annotate areas they didn't understand and seek clarification from the teacher outside of class. Where do pupils discover that When they start studying their notes, they don't make much sense. To help with memory, they can try writing down ideas in their own words or even drawing sketches, charts, or diagrams while taking notes. Finally, if a student finds it difficult to understand study notes, they can resolve the issue by clearing up any scribbles, fully expressing any concepts that have been truncated, or spelling important words correctly.

Constructing Study Sheets

Cheat sheets are another name for study sheets. With permission, students may bring a sheet of paper on test day that may aid in their memorization of the information they are tested on. Students make use of it should jot down particular equations, formulas, various data points, and other information that can come in use during the experiment. This sheet is not meant to take the place of research. Rather, it serves to refresh students' memories and serve as a reminder of difficult concepts or facts. Only those pupils who have adequately prepared for their exams can benefit from the technology. This sheet can be built by the student by first splitting it into columns. It is possible to label one column "Need to remember," another "Need to understand." Then, any formulas, equations, or other difficult-to-remember information that students might need to memorize in order to apply them are placed in the first column. Topics like "derivatives," "commodity markets," or anything else that will help the student retain a ton of knowledge that they couldn't fit on the sheet can be included in the second column.

It's a good idea to create subheadings for the items on this sheet. Students are given the opportunity to go into further information about the elements of a particular topic thanks to the subheadings. Making the most of the sheet is facilitated by the use of borders, arrows, and other visual aids. This also makes it easier to find the major elements of each write-up while editing.

5

CHAPTER 5: STUDY HABITS

In general, students' study habits vary. As pupils advance academically, some of these work well, while others are damaging to the learning process. The manner or strategy used for A student's academic pace should be matched with their study schedule. If students believe they study a lot but still don't perform well, they should probably reevaluate their routines and look for more efficient study techniques. On the other hand, students that perform very well should continue with such habits while also looking into new strategies to ensure even greater productivity in their studies.

Good Study Habits

Relax Your Mind to Study Well

Anxiety and an imbalanced emotional state impair a student's capacity to absorb information. handle and preserve fresh data.

The brain no longer forms connections. The heart rate increases, blood is sent to the limbs, and adrenaline levels skyrocket. All of this means that when studying, the brain effectively prevents access to higher processing, which makes it difficult to remember new knowledge. Regrettably, anxiety among students has increased to the point where an unprecedented proportion of pupils worldwide have reported having a mental health issue.

The following tested strategies are recommended to help pupils cope with this kind of mental strain. Finding the root cause of the issue is the first step towards solving it.

Keeping a regular notebook to record thoughts and feelings will help you recognize negative trends and stay away from certain triggers. of the nervousness. Either excessive coffee consumption late in the evening, irrational expectations, or insufficient sleep could be the cause. In addition, the student may try mindful training, which involves being conscious of thoughts and feelings and working on coping skills development. A student may also use seeking out social support as a coping mechanism for major stressors that could interfere with their ability to think clearly. Pupils with strong social networks are more balanced and healthier than those with little connections. This additional help might come from academic counselors, classmates, and teachers.

Because the mind and body are closely related, making healthy diet and exercise habits as well as getting enough sleep can already have a significant impact on mental condition. Foods that metabolize slowly, such whole wheat, lentils, and veggies, help lessen the anxiety that comes with blood sugar falls.

Taking On Moreover, mental attempts to remove oneself from unpleasant situations and obtain a fresh viewpoint might help manage anxiety and stress.

The basic way to do this is to have third-person conversations with ourselves. Though subtle, it has the power to significantly alter our perception of our circumstances and feelings. In addition, when things become too much to handle, students can also use active procrastination as a helpful approach. Although procrastination can be a student's worst enemy, it can also be employed as a strategy to put off a task while the learner concentrates on a more crucial one. This, therefore eliminates anything that may otherwise be a cause of stress for the overburdened student. The student postpones the assignment for a little while but continues to be productive by completing other important tasks on his or her to-do list. This action helps divert their attention from their anxiety.

Finally, organizing oneself by dividing academic assignments into manageable portions and establishing deadlines for yourself is another strategy students may use to calm their minds and control their anxiousness. The sense of helplessness is the main cause of worry. Correct organization gives the pupil a sense of control and makes them feel more at ease about the tasks at hand.

Adopt the Right Attitude

If students have a negative perspective of their academics and a poor attitude toward them, they will not be able to study successfully. Any student who wants to participate actively in the learning process needs to approach the classroom and learning environment with the appropriate mindset, not just toward the professors.

An educator has to be able to absorb the necessary techniques that support fostering a favorable attitude about a particular career. Even while there are challenges in the relationship between philosophy and learning, there are some areas where the teacher can concentrate and be sure that her efforts will be rewarded. The atmosphere in the classroom is becoming more and more important when determining how students feel about a certain training program. A learner's optimistic outlook indicates that it demonstrates that even in situations where a student has a negative attitude and perspective, the mental environment is still quite favorable to learning. It demonstrates that the atmosphere is not conducive to knowledge acquisition.

Rejection from peers and teachers is a significant factor that hinders a learner's progress in the educational process. Refusal can cause a student to focus in class and, in certain cases, even decide to drop out of the degree of education they are pursuing. The student may even want to transfer to a different school if their parents are able to pay the tuition, which would spare them from the same stigma.

The teacher or instructor should set up several methods that disclose a feeling of inclusion for the pupils. Making sure you maintain eye contact with the students is a simple way to establish acceptance and likeness. As an effective teacher, you should also focus on each of the classroom's four quadrants. You must make every effort to learn your students' names. Being able to identify your students by name gives you greater confidence and gratitude whenever you are speaking with them. Although it is customary for teachers to stand in front of the class, it is helpful to be able to roam around the room and interact with each student on a personal level. In a classroom while instruction is being conducted, When a teacher is appointed, they begin by asking questions. It is preferable if the instructor can observe how he or she handles the students' issues. Some pupils can seem to be asking obvious questions, so you don't have to ignore them. Even if a question may appear clear to a student, they may be having trouble finding the solution. To ensure that every student fully understands the lesson, give them plenty of time before moving on to something else.

Teachers should set activities that encourage pupils to take responsibility for their own learning in order to foster a good attitude in them. When students are working in groups on assignments, it's also crucial that they belong to tiny, controllable groupings. The group leader in the discussion groups must make sure that each member has a turn presenting to the class. These kinds of class presentations are how public speaking techniques are exercised. Certain group projects may also be extensive and encompass several study topics; for instance, the group leader should set tasks when working on a research project. A group member or two can do data gathering, another person can handle data cleaning, a third person can handle data analysis, and still another member can handle data discussion. Students can be particularly responsible to the group leader and for the overall outcomes of the task when they are given a specific allocation.

An additional strategy that is effective is when you take use of the pupils' natural curiosity. When students are unsure about how a task will appear on the other end, their attitude suffers and their attempts to finish the assignment are rendered useless. In order to improve the understandability of assigned duties, the instructor may provide an example of a completed task to support the assignment criterion. In order for students to embrace learning, they must be given the proper tools, the perfect amount of time, and clear directions on how to finish a task. They must also possess the necessary internal assets to believe that success is in their future. This encompasses aptitude, exertion, work complexity, and, to a certain degree, chance. The two most important factors of a learner's inspiration. Students who think they can complete a task with the help of their inner resource usually credit hard work for it.

Many students believe that they are strong in one area but weak in another, and they often credit talent or abilities for their accomplishments. The difficulty arises when a certain pupil starts to strongly believe that they can do a particular task, even though they are unable to. It is the instructor's duty to motivate students to persevere even if they lack skill in a particular area. Certain qualities come naturally to a person, while others can be acquired with nurturing and constant effort. When a pupil is ready, it is It is advised that you, as the teacher, initiate the effort to assist the pupil. On the other hand, the teacher ought to recognize that a pupil lacking talent may require a bit more time to understand. Thus, in this kind of situation, patience is essential.

Eat right

The type of food we put into our bodies affects how our brain functions. It performs numerous tasks nonstop every day, much like a computer. As such, it requires constant replenishment with glucose, a form of sugar, which serves as its fuel. The problem with glucose is that the body cannot keep it; instead, the bloodstream must carry it to the body.

It is imperative that students keep this in mind, particularly when they are focusing more on books. The body responds to improper fueling by having memory loss, insomnia, and difficulties solving problems.

In order for students to choose meals that will nourish their bodies, this section will examine how they eat their mind and facilitate a structured study regimen.

Removing harmful temptations from the menu, stocking only healthy options, or making healthy purchases are among suggested strategies. Due to hectic schedules, the student should also be very careful not to miss meals. The body need energy at all times of the day. On days when one has a busy schedule, one can take packed lunches rather than attempting to fit everything into one meal. Regarding alcohol, the pupil needs to use caution. Even worse are energy drinks like Red Bull, which are not FDA-approved and have high levels of caffeine, sugar, and other ingredients. Limit your intake to water just when you're thirsty. The student can choose meals high in simple sugars and protein when studying. Healthy meals high in protein maintain comparatively steady blood sugar levels and typically satisfy hunger more effectively than meals high in carbohydrates. Finally, every food group should be represented in the student's diet. Among them are 50% of a person's daily diet should consist of fruits and vegetables, with at least half of the grains they eat being whole. Because whole grains like brown rice and oatmeal include more fiber, they aid in preserving digestive health. Additional foods that are strong in protein include seeds, lean meat or poultry, beans, eggs, almonds, and fowl. Finally, dairy products should be ingested with low-fat or reduced-fat options. Control Your Stress Stress and anxiety can be brought on by the demands of a college education, jobs on campus, and social lives.

College life can be more enjoyable when stress is effectively managed, and it's a essential ability to possess.

Stress relievers that are appropriate for students should be speedy, easy to use, and somewhat related to their daily lives. While the student enjoys the process of learning new skills and talents, the stress relievers enable them to perform effectively and produce the greatest results.

One useful way to help a student feel less stressed is to encourage them to study in a clutter-free, distraction-free environment. When you consider an untidy location, the likelihood of not getting great results is really high. You can concentrate for longer periods of time when your study space is organized since it promotes inner calm.

A calm atmosphere helps students learn how to think positively and use affirmation techniques to talk to themselves in order to boost their self-esteem. Because of the way they think, an optimistic student has superior personal creative experiences. A pupil who is full of hope makes things better for themselves.

Exercise on a regular basis is one of the enjoyable activities that reduce stress.

Boost awareness and mental well-being as well as focus. Additionally helpful in enhancing sleep patterns, exercise also contributes to a further reduction in stress levels. Any workout that you find enjoyable is acceptable. While cardio workouts can be quite demanding and strenuous, yoga offers a novel and soothing kind of training. Any Exercise relieves tension in the body and mind, enabling you to study more effectively the next time.

Eating a good diet improves your overall health and cognitive function, which is beneficial for students. It has been demonstrated that a variety of foods and beverages can reduce tension and anxiety. Others, like coffee, will just make you feel more stressed. Certain foods, such as sunflower and pumpkin seeds, have exceptionally high magnesium content. Magnesium is a great modulator of emotions that could interfere with schooling, particularly in adolescence. Your body produces less cortisol, the stress hormone, when you drink black or green tea.

Target Problems and Prescribe the Solutions

Any work or assignment that needs to be completed is considered a problem. It will involve several steps, some of which may require the use of a certain, topic-specific methodology. Developing and mastering the ability to solve problems is a crucial talent for students to succeed in their academic endeavors. The first step in approaching assignments or challenges in the academic world is to define the task and ascertain what is necessary in the particular circumstance. You must establish a clear hierarchy of needs on what should come first and what can wait to be addressed at a later date.

Subsequently, the pupil formulates a suitable strategy to tackle the assignment.

Having knowledge from comparable previous assignments, the learner is provided with guidance on how to approach the task. Setting goals entails determining what has to be done and by when. A detailed action plan with deadlines is drawn out, outlining the sequence in which each work is to be completed. The next step is to get going, keep an eye on performance in relation to goals, and periodically update the plan to account for unforeseen developments.

After then, performance is assessed to see how successfully objectives were met and to record lessons gained for use in upcoming tasks. Determining the task and giving it to the pupils is the most important step in this procedure.

Pupils who take the time to determine which assignment has

the best probability of producing superior results produce really good odds of success for oneself.

You are expanding on an issue when you take the time to complete a task, which cuts down on the amount of time it will take you to find a solution. Every problem has a variety of solutions, therefore the more time you choose to attempt and explain the issue, the shorter the time it takes to find a solution. You will either take longer to tackle the problem or come up with mediocre solutions if you jump in too quickly without taking the time to grasp it. Finding the optimal answer requires time and effort. But in order to find the optimal answer, it's also essential to keep the following in mind: It is necessary to have a concept of what the ideal solution would be; options that cannot be completed by the deadline should be avoided; it is also advisable to talk with colleagues to further debate alternatives. Finally, evaluating the benefits and drawbacks of summarized solutions will improve the calibre of the chosen final solution.

Steps to Easier Learning

Self-directed learning, usually referred to as independent learning, may be extremely difficult, even for students who are strong self-motivators. Being open to learning, establishing objectives for yourself, participating in the process, and assessing your progress are all examples of natural learning strategies.

The learner ought to assess themselves in terms of their present circumstances, the study practices that work for her, as well as the most dependable home and school study support system. In addition, you can assess the student's learning process independently and beyond their experience. Some pupils are more equipped to study than others; these individuals tend to be self-sufficient, possess exceptional organizational skills, and exhibit strong self-discipline. In addition, the student possesses the ability to speak clearly and engage in self-analysis and introspection. When you offer such students advice or feedback, they readily take it as a beneficial addition to their lives and the educational process in general.

Choosing the appropriate training or learning environment is the second crucial stage for learners objectives and successfully conveying them to the students. The teacher and the student must agree on the objectives. The creation of contracts as a point of reference is advised in order to foster a clear grasp of learning objectives. The objectives of the research unit, the well-built structure, and the order of the pertinent activities must all be included in the agreement. You must also choose and establish a deadline for the student to follow in order for them to finish a particular activity. The necessary resources are essential to achieving each of the objectives. Establishing a transparent and comprehensible grading system and assessing every target you have established is also essential.

To assist, the instructor can schedule meetings and sessions with the student. to assist in providing guidance as the learner advances through the task.

Reaching the most appropriate learning process engagement for the student is the third phase. To be able to provide pertinent counsel and direction regarding the study strategy being used, a teacher must be aware of the unique needs of each student. One option is to use a surface approach, which consists of memorizing the material covered in a particular study unit. In a different setting, a depth approach is necessary, which entails comprehending concepts, applying information to novel circumstances, and overall learning more than the unit requires.

Finally, there is a methodical approach to education that focuses on obtaining high grades or scores. With this method, the student simply learns pertinent information regarding an impending test. Through a process of going over previous exam papers, the student commits the information to memory without trying to think beyond what they can see.

The learner can participate in a self-reflection and self-evaluation process as the fourth and last step in this self-directed learning process. The student's progress in the study unit and the objectives they have set should be the main topics of the self-evaluation. The assessment process ought to involve frequent discussions with the teacher, continuously seeking feedback, and reflecting on achievements.

Technique of Spaced Repetition

One type of learning called spaced repetition is repeating data that indicates a pupil is attempting to memorize in order to flash it out later on when responding to questions, like in a final exam. In order to employ this study strategy efficiently, students need first review the new study materials, then take some right tie and go over it numerous times. After learning, it's helpful to acquaint yourself with the subject matter or study unit before thinking about study tools. Put another way, the review aids in the construction of a pattern that helps you remember the material and makes room in your memory bank for the new knowledge.

The student's ability to conceive and make connections between ideas and principles is improved since the knowledge they remember in their minds grows into larger chunks rather than distinct informational fragments. In order to employ this strategy for more natural learning, a student must first make sure that the notes or information they originally read are reviewed within 24 hours. Try looking away from the book or the material you are reading to see if you can remember it. It is the most effective way to find out if you can recall the main ideas from a certain unit of study.

The pupil needs to understand that this is not a recall when they reread. It's likely that knowledge is not being retained in your memory when you reread it. Therefore, it is essential that you practice remembering the material after reading.

Step two is to set the notes away and make an effort to remember the details without delay. One day following the initial evaluation, this should be completed. Either strolling at your own pace or just sitting down can help you recall the knowledge.

The learner can also make this exercise more efficient by creating flashcards with the major concepts and then testing themselves right away.

The next step is to try fast, recalling the study content at certain times throughout the day. As you have more experience, you can extend the ranges to 24 hours a day for a few days. In addition, the recalling may take place in a matter of days or, over time, even months. It's likely that you will already have the information in the back of your head by the time it gets intervals today. The type of recollect Periods can occur during lunch break, the walk home at the end of the day, or even in between breaks when moving from one class to the next.

To find out if they can correctly identify the solution, one should test or quiz themselves. This is a good place for flashcards, as the reverse may be used to find the answers. The final stage in mastering this strategy is to get out all of the material a few days prior to the test and begin reviewing or studying it. One week of study is a tried-and-true method of getting ready for a review. This gave the pupil the opportunity to retain and solidify the information once more and gave their brain a chance to comprehend the thoughts or ideas.

Bad Study Habits

cramming for tests In order to succeed academically, students must cultivate effective study techniques or habits. But for the majority of students, cramming becomes a habit when test time approaches. This behavior or study style is typical of disorganized, last-minute pupils who are easily distracted. When a student spends a lot of time trying to memorize particular study units, it is known as cramming.

Cramming aims to quickly acquire knowledge while paying little attention to understanding the material. Some students think that cramming is the best way to study because they still perform well on tests when they do it.

The pupil has the option to stay up late and then wake up early the following morning to review, and they claim to be putting in a lot of effort at work.

A prevalent habit among students who enjoy last-minute revision techniques is cramming. The drawback of cramming is that there is a slim chance that the student will recall the material after they take the test.

One study technique that professors should discourage their pupils from using to master any subject is cramming because it interferes with the learning process. A student who crams loses the chance to acquire and comprehend anything new, squandering a valuable educational opportunity. Getting good grades in the study units is the main goal of cramming.

The fact that cramming just makes things more stressful is one of the main reasons it is ineffective. Stress negatively impacts a student's capacity to focus, which makes getting ready for the test a difficult chore.

The student must give up more sleep in exchange for more study time.

Inadequate sleep or irregular sleeping habits lead to subpar work output.

When a student spends time reviewing material for a test the next morning, the brain stores it in the short-term memory area and makes it readily available in short bursts of time. When a student uses cramming to acquire good grades, they forget what they learned and then cram for the next test, which makes it difficult for them to retain the knowledge for long.

Students can utilize the spaced learning approach discussed in the previous part under to study without cramming. In order to better understand the content, the student looks over the study materials and information over an extended period of time. The student's ideas and the concepts covered in a particular unit might be continuously connected in the mind. Recalling the material becomes lot easier when you make an effort to increase your knowledge and understanding of a given subject.

Study plans are also quite effective at dividing the entire amount of material to be studied into manageable portions within a set amount of time. In contrast to cramming, the study plan provides guidance on what to do next, which helps reduce confusion.

Finally, and perhaps most importantly, study schedules help

students retain information that they can use in the future.

Consuming Energy Drinks

Students that study insane hours at night and have end-of-term exams have developed a culture of poor study habits and lack focus. Use of energy drinks to enhance academic performance is one of these unhealthy practices. Blood vessel function has been known to be impacted by energy drinks. Moreover, chemicals linked to the emergence of high blood pressure can be released more often when energy drinks are consumed. An general sense of exhaustion is also exacerbated by stress. When exam season approaches, students who struggle with stress and sleep deprivation reach for these beverages. They accept the drinks and experience a pleasant surge in energy. The issue arises when the students begin to feel hangover-like or have headaches a few hours later. Right now At a certain moment, a student decides that he or she needs more energy and, in an attempt to gain more strength, decides to drink more energy drinks, adding to the cycle of repetition. Users fail to realize that studying calls for sustained focus, which is impossible to do when under a lot of stress. The strict and sensible advise for these pupils is to adhere to the regimen, which entails attending classes and focusing. A student can perform well on tests if they take their studies seriously, eat healthily, exercise, and get adequate sleep. Relying on energy alone causes a student's body to have an underlying issue that completely adds to exhaustion. For a student to be healthy, it is also essential that they prepare meals that are high in nutrients. Consuming complex carbohydrates and lean proteins improves general health and provides you with sustained high-energy levels. Fruit consumption is crucial since fruits are high in fiber, vitamins, and minerals. The fruits support the students' healthy digestion and general well-being.

Lack of water consumption is another prevalent cause of weariness, which has led to a student obsession with energy drinks. Dehydration is a symptom that other essential systems are also experiencing a slowdown, and this appears to be the cause. to experience exhaustion and laziness. If you don't drink much water, you should start by investing in a large water container, which will help you monitor how much fluid you consume. There is extremely little likelihood of using energy drinks when your daily water intake is enough.

Exercise is still one of the safest ways to increase energy.

Dopamine and serotonin, two feel-good brain chemicals, can be increased through exercise. The body's ability to produce more is much enhanced while these hormone levels are rising, which improves both mental and physical function.

Getting By on Junk Food

Poor diet has been shown to have an impact on a student's health and, consequently, their performance in school. Even if they are aware of the dietary requirements for their bodies, college students also gain the freedom to select the kind, quantity, and optimal timing of their meals. These students have a range of options available to them at reasonable prices at the campus canteens and dining facilities. Students may use their free will to form unhealthy eating habits that are difficult to break or healthy eating habits that are easy to maintain.

The main issue is that students now place a higher priority on flavor and convenience.

It follows that the majority of the time, people make bad eating selections.

As far as feasible, the study space should be calm and distraction-free. Students frequently stroll and even sit around campus When students are staring down at their handheld gadgets in class, are they doing so to study or are they just using them for recreational activities like updating Facebook profiles or tweeting? Most of them become sidetracked from interacting with classmates and may not even participate in educational activities. Some students think they may use these devices inappropriately in class while multitasking and participating actively. Instructors can improve the learning environment by monitoring student distractions during study sessions.

Sometimes hunger or weariness are the sole issues. Making sure the student has a nutritious meal before starting their studies is the answer.

The pupil can also learn to moderate their ideas while studying by organizing a mental shift activity, like listening to music, to help them concentrate. Try recording conflicting and diverting ideas in a journal or post-it note and putting them away for later. In this manner, the student will presumably be able to set them away till they are finished working and won't forget them. Lastly, to avoid distractions and hold oneself accountable for their study goals, students should look for a companion or fellow student.

To do this, study with a friend or in a group and hold each other accountable for staying on course.

Ineffective Time Management

One of the most important things for any effort in life to succeed is time management. Pupils need to possess the ability of properly managing time by creating routines for your interests, socializing, napping, and study time. There are certain pupils who are masters at managing their time.

They consistently arrive on time, avoid using the snooze button, and turn in their work ahead of schedule. Some people have poor time management skills and leave tasks till the last minute, which causes them to feel stressed out when they have to catch up. These students struggle to strike a balance between their academic load, test scores, and extracurricular activities like athletics, and they ultimately fail on all fronts.

Pupils who fall behind in their coursework have a harder time comprehending and applying new information. Ultimately, they produce a regrettable academic performance in a vicious loop. Ineffective time management leads to stress, which in turn causes learning and grades to suffer.

Students who struggle with time management tend to prioritize other things above their sleep. Ultimately, this leads to exhaustion and potential health problems. Unintentionally developing unhealthy eating habits is another effect of ineffective time management. When students neglect breakfast due to staying up late to fulfill deadlines for their studies, they may turn to unhealthy fast food or junk food. In addition to constantly being late for appointments and classes, unmanageable students also end up coming across as unprofessional.

When a student frequently fails to arrive on time, both teachers and fellow students take notice. At last, a pupil who is Poor time management causes one to consistently put off duties, which makes one appear sloppy. They turn their assignments with typos and grammatical faults. Tests are typically assigned early in the semester by instructors to allow students enough time to finish them. Effective time management will guarantee that the caliber of work.

6

CHAPTER 6: CONCENTRATION AND STUDYING

How Concentration Impacts Studies

One way to define concentration is being aware of the appropriate things at the appropriate times. Better yet, it is the capacity to focus one's thoughts in the specific direction desired. This entails being mindful of a extended amount of time to absorb all the knowledge required to complete a task and see it through to the very conclusion. Pupils that possess a high degree of concentration are capable of overcoming various distractions and behaviors that result in a loss of focus. They'll work better, faster, and more comfortably. By being attentive and ultimately reaching an ideal studying condition, they will ace tests, assignments, and classes.

It might be difficult to focus on one thing at a time, especially when the subject or content is not a preferred. Academic success is also impeded in areas where level lags. The following are blatant indicators that someone is not attentive or has not been paying close attention. When a learner experiences overwhelming feelings from routine daily tasks, finds it difficult to concentrate on simple tasks, struggles with effective communication or carrying on a normal conversation, finds it difficult to stay awake and resists impulses, finds it difficult to form thoughts or feels as though their mind is racing, finds it difficult to stay organized, and finds it difficult to make important decisions. All of these ought to make a student feel compelled to take the necessary actions to put themselves back in the proper frame of mind so they can concentrate and work well.

Still, Focused concentration can be utilized to hack even the most boring moments or sessions with a defined purpose and useful skills.

All that's needed to improve attention is to make advantage of your own inherent abilities. This can be done methodically by the learner, who can then try to manage their focus and master it with minimal effort. Work on it on a regular basis and set realistic goals for what can be accomplished in the allotted time.

Concentration levels can vary based on a number of factors, including how engaging the activity at hand is, the learner's capacity to solve a particular problem, their physical and emotional states when working in teams, their commitment to the task, and the availability of supportive environments. that is practically distraction-free. When a learner has the correct mentality and is able to control these aspects, they will find that they can focus better and shut out irrelevant ideas and activities. Acquiring proficiency in concentration is a talent. Furthermore, learning a talent requires practice. It takes practice to improve concentration using the techniques used. It is likely that one may start to notice changes in a few days. Following four to six weeks of instruction, the student will see a noticeable difference.

Reasons for Inability to Focus

Our capacity for concentration can be enhanced and is influenced by a number of different circumstances. For most people, concentration comes naturally, but for others, it does not. Many pupils experience challenges having a serious difficulty concentrating, remaining focused, or maintaining attention. It's normal to feel distracted or absentminded from time to time. However, if it continues, it can be a sign of other serious issues that need to be found and treated. Understanding the causes of low focus is crucial to treating and resolving the issue. Different students can learn to concentrate, and it may become a skill they enjoy and find easy to use. Addressing the source or reason of the poor concentration as well as the other things you can discover will be part of the process of enhancing concentration.

When a student attempts to study for an extended period of time without distractions, they are likely to focus poorly. This research a method of learning known as "marathon studying," which is ineffective when long-term memory, profound focus, and correct comprehension are needed.

One of the main causes of this issue is stress, which is known to raise blood pressure, create mental exhaustion, impair immunity, and, in the worst case scenario, start depression. It is challenging to concentrate or think clearly when the brain is worn out. Inadequate sleep and rest can also affect how well the brain functions.

Not getting enough sleep can also impair focus and cause mental fog. It is advised to make sure you obtain seven or eight hours of sleep per night.

Whether or whether a student has poor concentration is

also influenced by their diet. Foods high in vitamin B-12 are recognized to help an appropriate brain function. Thus, insufficient of the same can result in difficulty focusing. Food allergies may also be the source of a brain condition that impairs acute concentration. In addition to being uncomfortable, hunger can impair focus. As previously mentioned, a deficiency in nutrition alters brain function; as a result, the experience of hunger will make it difficult to concentrate. Physical pain is another feeling that interferes with concentration. It is possible to become distracted when in pain. Another emotional condition that makes it difficult for a student to focus is worry.

The learner's surroundings, including the people and locations they are in, have an impact on their ability to focus. A loss of focus is often caused by distractions. The capacity of the learner superior focus over others will affect one's ability to concentrate. A few students excel at it more than others.

The stability of the learner's home or social milieu is closely tied to the environment. Some families openly communicate their financial struggles and local problems to their student children. This type of learner may experience overwhelm, which impairs focus. Certain dysfunctions including drug addiction, drunkenness, and domestic violence can lead to conflicts.

Boredom resulting from meaningless and unmotivating activities is another major offender. Sometimes a student may fail to see how a particular course or their academics relate to their career objectives. Some don't actually give a damn about receiving a college degree, and as a result, they struggle to attend lectures, take notes, finish homework, and even study for tests. Lack of interest is linked to a lack of motivation. The student chooses to stick with studying certain things but loses interest in others; he or she focusses well in some lecturers but not in others.

There exist additional potential reasons for inadequate concentration, which are associated with the mental health or psychological well-being of students. These ailments include neurological disorders that impede brain function and impact learning, memory, and concentration, brain traumas, and cognitive impairment, which is defined by developmental delays or impairments.

Another mental impulsive illness is attention-deficit/hyperactivity disorder (ADHD). This makes learning and remembering difficult for students. It can be challenging to focus or concentrate when other mental health issues, like sadness and anxiety, go untreated. Memory loss and focus are also impacted by concussions and other brain traumas. But these are typically only transient. A major impairment to concentration can also be caused by vision issues, such as farsightedness. Students who find themselves squinting frequently or who suffer from continuous headaches should have a medical examination of their eyes done.

Chronic mental tiredness, which can persist for up to six months, is caused by other medical disorders that are typically linked to weariness, inflammation, or a shift in glucose levels. Brain fog can also result from anemia, diabetes, multiple sclerosis, Alzheimer's disease, lupus, migraines, and dehydration, among other medical issues.

Ways to Boost Focus

The ability to focus is a critical skill that impacts everything a student does. They will learn more in class and do better on tests if they consistently use this skill and maintain the proper focus and concentration. According to experts, there are three stages of concentration: the first, which happens five minutes after a student begins reading or performing a task, requires the least amount of focus as it is readily distracted.

The medium concentration follows, which may require up to five minutes.

It starts when a pupil becomes more attentive and is only distracted by face-to-face contacts, such as a siren, loud noise, or ringing phone. At last, we reach the state of maximal concentration, during which a highly focused and every diversion is disregarded. The process may take up to an hour, following which a little pause is required because of a decrease in focus.

An full study session shouldn't run longer than two hours, including the study breaks. The brain will be able to process and assimilate the material more easily as a result. Prior to regaining maximal focus, one should return to the first two levels of concentration when they become distracted. In order to achieve practical study, a student must make sure their study space is free from frequent distractions. If a student finds a specific subject tedious, they can take a short break from it and return later to finish up their studies. This effectively increases level of focus.

When a student starts an assignment knowing exactly what they want to get done, they are more likely to focus only on that one task at hand. They will be able to focus more effectively during that particular study session if they have this clear and distinct goal. It is easier to reduce outside distractions when one's goal is so obvious.

Using time management techniques is essential for enhancing focus as well. A common internal diversion experienced by students is the concern that they will not have enough time to complete their study assignments. While working on one task, others will be considering their other due assignments. A study regimen will help the student be completely focused while they work on every task.

Another strategy for improving concentration is to create a good learning environment. Among other things, this entails locating a quiet study area, blocking calls, shutting off the TV, and reserving the desktop for studying purposes in order to remove outside distractions that could impair your focus.

Learning to multitask less is a great way for students to improve their study focus. A person who performs numerous tasks at once is said to be multitasking. Multitasking is when a student answers a phone call and types an essay. Multitasking also includes reviewing a course chapter and watching a game on television. The students' continuous attention switching between tasks will have an impact on their focus during the procedure.

Developing and implementing useful study techniques is another way to approach this issue. The learner must be able to relate to the items for which they already have consent and integrate a particular component into the larger picture. They will be inspired to stay focused by this. Concentration is significantly simpler when a learner is actively engaged in the task at hand. Whether a person is a visual or auditory learner should be determined on an individual basis.

Nonetheless, since memory traces will be stronger, it is advised to use both. Subsequently, the student ought to select subjects that are both engaging and easy to study. This ought to be mixed in with less controversial subjects fascinating. The student should evaluate the material he has learned and get ready for the next session every thirty minutes. This will be advantageous because the student will have divided the activity into manageable chunks that can be promptly assessed to determine the caliber of work produced.

Another tactic for improving academic performance is to address academic issues head-on. The student might meet with a tutor to discuss concerns or ask for help with the tasks required to attain academic objectives. When students believe in their skills and future, it is easier for them to reduce distractions and increase focus. The student will benefit from this kind of instruction by developing a positive action focus. where, rather than being concerned Instead than thinking negatively about things like their dislikes or worries, the student concentrates on their goals and the steps they are taking to get there.

Other strategies for enhancing focus include encouraging students to take good care of their bodies through appropriate diet, exercise, and rest. This effectively conveys the idea that the body and the mind are intricately linked.

If the student has seen a continuous inability to focus, they want to think about obtaining a physical examination. This will allow them to determine the learner's mental health, food, degree of physical activity, and whether or not they are using any drugs. Blood testing can also show if there are any infections, inflammations, nutritional deficits, or abnormal glucose levels all of which could have an impact on acute focus. Avoiding excessive alcohol and caffeine, obtaining at least 8 hours of sleep, exercising, and boosting intake of proteins, fruits, vegetables, and healthy fats are some tried-and-true home treatments for enhancing focus and attention.

7

CHAPTER 7: CREATING AND MAINTAINING A STUDY LEARNING CULTURE

According to a number of studies, every kid deserves the opportunity to learn in a supportive setting. Many are known to struggle in their classes, develop self-doubt, or experience difficult times focusing on your academics. In general, education as a whole can be highly intimate. Whatever the cause of a student's difficulties in a particular course, stress can be effectively managed provided the student is in a supportive learning environment. It goes without saying that quality work must be included in order to foster a healthy learning environment.

A positive learning environment takes into account a number of factors, as discussed in the discussion that follows:

To assist students feel safe, they need to provide a feeling of order beside the instructor. A teacher can effectively manage a classroom when they are equipped with relevant content, as it boosts their confidence in the classroom setting.

Every pupil requires a sound framework. It is the duty of the instructor to provide a high standard of academic and social discipline through outstanding composition. From the very start of the educational contact, the expectations must be established. Establishing standards early on helps prevent additional issues, such as disrespect, from developing as the children get to know the teacher. In a classroom setting, numerous hands-on activities and assignments should be used to educate pupils safe and effective practices.

When an educator receives students should figure up a method to make up the work they missed because not all of them were able to attend class. Simple actions like rearrangement of the classroom might help the teacher gain attention and enhance concentration. Students are free to set up seminars, group discussions, or cooperative learning activities. Group talks improve the students' overall comprehension of the program or course by enabling them to view things from fresh and distinct angles.

The teacher needs to keep in mind that pupils have psychological and physical needs, just like responsible adults have. Among the needs are those for freedom, love, belonging, and security. The fascinating thing is that each kid aspires to fulfill all these needs each and every time, not simply when they're necessary. A happy class that eagerly anticipates the course will arise when a teacher or instructor is able to meet all of these needs. Additionally, there aren't many discipline situations at this level, making learning fluid and simple to advance.

Instructors should also make sure they are aware of their students' interests and passions for extracurricular activities, as well as their personalities, learning preferences, and cultural backgrounds. It is simpler for the teacher to connect with the

CHAPTER 7: CREATING AND MAINTAINING A STUDY LEARNING CULTURE

class and successfully involve them in the learning process when there is understanding. Among the creative methods they can use for this are carried out through team-building exercises, frequent meetings, learning and personality tests completed by the students, and participation in extracurricular activities.

In addition, they can educate themselves about their own cultures and areas of interest. Lastly, they can assign journals to students for review and eventual grading.

A very related strategy to the one mentioned above is getting the pupils to know their instructor or teacher. The idea that pupils develop a specific instructor is greatly controlled by having a proper comprehension of your instructor. Currently, the instructor's only means of influencing a student's perception is by offering them fresh or unique experiences. In the first week of the semester, the instructor may administer an exam on themself. This test would include topics that are more individual as opposed to professional. Later, the teacher talks over the solutions with the class. The instructor is willing to provide photos of their hometown, family, and other stuff.

When a teacher and student are on the same level, it gives the pupils confidence and reassurance that they are speaking with a regular person. When a teacher wishes to appear distant and unapproachable from their students, it is a disadvantage. For students to regard their professors as mentors and role models, they must really connect with them. An alternative to the quiz would be for the teacher to tell the class about themselves, their values, and what they will or won't do not perform for pupils, and what kind of work will you anticipate from them?

Teachers require frequent opportunity to demonstrate and consider their methods of instruction. Every time they succeed, it increases their intrinsic motivation. The task for school leadership is to attempt and establish a number of venues and stages where teachers can present their methods and possibilities. This kind of opportunity not only assists the pupils in learning, but it also significantly boosts the teachers' competitiveness and self-esteem overall. The institution should provide several avenues for students to engage with other outside specialists in order to do this. Teacher exchange programs are a method that enables a teacher to communicate with an alternative class. A teacher working with a separate class can identify problems or strengths in a group of students or in a single kid that a regular teacher would miss. Other educational demonstration activities should be included in the teaching seminars that different institutions should plan and conduct. Teachers can discuss the difficulties they encounter and receive helpful advice and resources in these kinds of forums. Teachers are impacted by these demonstrative activities in two ways. Working together to develop classes allowed them to gain knowledge and understanding.

The beneficial impact of the teachers' input is a noteworthy and significant outcome. Positive feedback from students makes teachers feel more confident. instructors and perhaps kindle a love or urge to enroll in more courses.

Additionally, it is a good idea for the school to create systems that can boost students' feelings of accomplishment, particularly for non-title teachers. Teachers with more experience or training might offer their services as mentors to aspiring educators at a particular educational level. Instructors with more expertise should also assist upcoming professionals in that industry by providing them with opportunities to gain better exposure and by sharing their resource materials. Encouraging teachers to participate in these kinds of events is crucial since it even gives senior instructors a sense of pride because they

CHAPTER 7: CREATING AND MAINTAINING A STUDY LEARNING CULTURE

experience the recognition of the prospective experts. As a result, institutional learning and service quality are improved. The attempt by aspiring professionals to learn from seasoned educators is another tactic that might enhance the learning environment in a facility. In these situations, young professionals also need to be careful not to adjust to educational institutions that can be out of date given how quickly they are developing now. at order to raise standards and improve the learning environment at the institutions, teachers with more experience are also placed in a position where they may critically evaluate their own abilities and share them with others.

Another tactic for fostering a learning culture in classrooms is the creation of a set of circumstances that support learning in the context of the teacher's career. Teachers are better able to understand the precise purpose and worth of the careers they are interested in when administrators integrate learning into their work lives. To do this, schools cultivate an environment that welcomes creativity and makes instructors believe that, despite the challenges of their work, teaching is immensely fulfilling. Put another way, the understanding that teaching is more than just what they do for a living motivates teachers to educate. They see the value in teaching and work to foster the ideal environment and culture of learning.

A teacher needs to identify a long-term cause that will inspire an inner drive for improvement. An amazing illustration would be if a teacher expressed their desire to see students exhibit even greater professionalism than they do. When a teacher is passionate about what they do, they actively look for possibilities for their students and follow up to make sure they are complying. For an educator, nothing provides greater motivation than the profound realization that the lessons my pupils acquire will have an impact on their lives in the future. Teachers who receive feedback from an instructor during their training eventually come to believe that the comments and suggestions are helpful. The instructor becomes ecstatic, content, self-assured, and eager to teach. Other educators have to relearn and unlearn their methods and talents. that they may cling to and recognize at that time as the sole tricks capable of working wonders. The process of unlearning entails a professional rejuvenation, which may foster a congenial atmosphere that facilitates the development of novel professional practices between educators and students.

The open and sharing method is flexible in encouraging teacher collaboration, which improves the educational experience for students in institutions. Because of this, it is essential that you foster a sense of trust so that the instructors feel very confident even as they attempt to employ various strategies.

The many strategies contribute to the students' learning experience being unforgettable. Organizations that value and comprehend their educators should not rely on top-down control measures to provide direction and mentor the educators. Conversely, these schools implement compassionate practices that provide care for both teachers and pupils.

A school can create incredibly effective learning cultures and systems if they can alter the way teachers view their own learning. The teachers agree that having an open communication system and a selfless support network makes it easier for them to create a very happy work and learning environment. The idea that teaching and learning are not exclusive has to sink in for all educators. Teachers can become more astute and perceptive if they can enroll in a course while they are employed. Then and only then can they work to improve instruction and the educational process for their pupils. Creative systems for teacher learning are changing how people view education and learning.

Teachers need to know that learning is not more labor.

However, it makes their instruction far more engaging and successful. Once you have a certain amount of knowledge from prior experience, you may use learning as a great way to pinpoint your areas of weakness and gain fresh perspectives on your line of work. The teachers keep moving forward with the striking idea that becoming familiar with the local way of life will provide them with lots of chances to demonstrate their teaching abilities. Young teachers benefit from this professional development provided by schools, which is attentive in their ongoing quest for improved instruction that prioritizes the needs of students. The purpose of the teachers' visit is to help them comprehend the importance that instruction imparts. When students observe what their role models are doing, they become more interested in seeking knowledge on their own. Their role models play a crucial part in motivating them to take risks, cultivate a strong desire to adapt, and adopt a more creative teaching approach. Using this method increases a teacher's willingness and motivation to positively impact their pupils' lives.

Positive relationships with students and even among themselves can be fostered via the use of games and activities in the classroom.

These games are ideal for splitting up student groups in a classroom because they are mostly cooperative and non-competitive. when there are no cliques or social groups Giving timid pupils who might be relatively new to the class a strong sense of belonging helps them feel comfortable and included. Because the games deviate from the norm, attending class is enjoyable. Since many students find playing these games in class to be interesting, they can increase a level's attendance to the maximum. Some pupils come to look forward to the kind of class that is really enjoyable.

rewarding with cash incentives and other rewards with the express intent of dictating how students should complete their assignments in order to weaken their desire to learn. Additionally, it complicates relationships and teaches kids that nothing is worth doing without compensation. What the teacher should emphasize is that every human being possesses a distinct reward system under brain control. A more practical way to improve a learning culture is to celebrate students' accomplishments rather than using rewards to get them to concentrate on their studies. A celebration is an impromptu gathering to honor accomplishments. First, the class sets a goal, and then their progress is tracked and recorded. Following every evaluation, the teacher talks with the student about their specific methods, routines, and approaches to success.

To have an even better assessment, they also go over what they have learnt and what needs to be done. When the objective is reached, the teacher celebrates in recognition of the students' work and growth.

An instructor might also foster trust by refraining from passing judgment on their students. Pupils who experience judgment or Labeled people become less motivated to participate in active learning. But identifying and passing judgment on students is a sign of a teacher who is abdicating their duty to shape them. It doesn't address the fundamental causes of behavior, which can be addressed immediately and with less time and effort. In addition to the aforementioned, the teacher might gain the pupils' trust by showing vulnerability. This entails owning up to errors, which demonstrates one's humanity and approachability. The learner can also clearly see that anyone can make mistakes and that doing so is perfectly acceptable. Accepting that mistakes are a necessary part of learning allows pupils to develop their assurance. Being vulnerable allows a kid to cultivate a growth mindset, which quickly spreads throughout the school. In order to improve, the pupils accept their errors and draw lessons from them.

Additionally, the teacher can establish a routine in which students greet each other at the door and get to know each other as soon as they walk into the classroom. Making eye contact and extending a verbal hello helps them do this. Every student will benefit from this in terms of a human connection, and it also conveys to them that you, the teacher, are concerned about them as individuals.

Setting high standards for pupils aids in forming the other extra tactics and approaches that support the development of a culture of learning and study among them The academic and social attributes of a pupil. When a teacher establishes expectations, the pupils have to put in a lot of effort to follow the guidelines. Students are being urged to interact positively and show support for one another. This is significant because it fosters a positive and collaborative classroom culture. Furthermore, it is imperative that kids feel empowered and have a voice in the classroom.

8

CHAPTER 8: CONTINUOUS LEARNING DEVELOPMENT

The nature of teaching in workplaces and schools has remained mostly unchanged over the past many centuries. Throughout the initial years of our lives, pupils attend traditional schools where they are taught a set curriculum of subjects. The learner is able to have a foundational set of skills thanks to the standard selection of disciplines. A student can pursue further postsecondary or advanced education, or they can obtain a primary career with the requisite abilities.

The educational system is always changing in order to remain comprehensive and add new levels. The new levels assist the children in achieving both high literacy and respectable educational standards. The graduates must should consider carefully how we receive our education given the rapid changes that the world is undergoing. The ideas you work with and the kind of duties you perform are directly impacted by the developments occurring throughout the world.

Changes in the world have an impact on how you conduct your life as well.

CHAPTER 8: CONTINUOUS LEARNING DEVELOPMENT

Stated differently, it is necessary to embrace a new worldview. Only a small elite has ever been able to attend traditional schools. But as the industrial revolution got underway, education began to grow significantly. Europe is the one who starts the primary school model's adoption. Over the course of the next 150 years, the primary school model was adopted by Japan and the rest of the western world. Getting a fundamental These primary school models set goals for children in reading, writing, essential singing, and religious comprehension. The elementary school model incorporates more subject areas after a period of advancement. Including the other areas of knowledge has turned into a way to produce more people with higher-level skills in keeping with the technological advancements.

The system is turning into one of the tools for producing better people since the establishment of democracies and a central government. Improved abilities in all facets of professionalism are necessary for future progress. Since the first part of the 20th century, secondary schools have become the standard as a result of the desire to acquire superior abilities. But these days, this might not be the case. be adequate given the level of automation and the increased demand of today's jobs. A sizeable percentage of today's young pupils find work in nonexistent settings.

The labor force of today operates in a variety of industries, performing new and in-development tasks. One instance is the field of building mobile software, where the process began less than 20 years ago. Online marketing and data mining are two more emerging fields. One of the challenges associated with these emerging categories of work is that educators must equip their students to find work in industries that have not yet developed or established. That can only occur in a setting where learning never stops. sometimes known as "lifelong learning."

This entails engaging in a range of activities to learn a variety of subjects outside of the classroom. This approach's main goal is to use one's knowledge and abilities to become a contributing member of society as well as an active teaching professional who can adapt to a variety of settings. Such a teacher constantly gains knowledge from a variety of sources, shares it, and inspires other professionals to follow their own learning objectives. In the past, consultants who specialized in lifelong or continuous learning models would arrive at the start of the school year and spend a predetermined amount of time introducing the new curriculum. Later, the consultant gives the teachers a ton of instructional resources that assist in putting the curriculum into practice.

It's fascinating to see how the instructors begin instructing the pupils after that, leaving the teaching resources on the shelf in their offices. The teachers attend class and carry on teaching in the same manner because they won't complete their assignments and learn the material. This method of ongoing improvement was unable to bring about a long-lasting shift in instructional strategies. In actuality, teachers and students are similar in that both require multiple training sessions in order to fully grasp the topic and apply the newly acquired teaching tools.

There is a paradigm change in the current educational system that encompasses learning new skills and the process of gaining knowledge. When educators possess special abilities, They are able to take on and complete new assignments.

The benefit of this kind of structure is that it enables professors to provide fresh perspectives to the professional fields that already exist. In addition to their ability to adjust to a constantly changing environment, instructors also continuously acquire

CHAPTER 8: CONTINUOUS LEARNING DEVELOPMENT

new concepts that are critical in today's classrooms.

The learning process is easier to access thanks to technology. To comprehend the current developments in education, teachers do not need to re-enroll in college or any other higher education establishment. The teachers have the option to learn new things, pace themselves, and save time. Online courses are a reasonably priced way to access the new experience. Free training programs are also offered by some employers, particularly for the personnel of the government as well as a few other organizations. There are a ton of online courses available that offer a wide range of skill specializations. The benefit is that one can obtain certificates for various qualifications by specializing in talents.

However, it's a concerning tendency that these courses are only open to those with professional work experience in addition to a higher education degree. There are rumors that a number of institutions that stand to gain from ongoing development are not utilizing these chances.

As much as you would like to hold them responsible, you must acknowledge that many of these educators are ignorant of the many organizations, the courses and programs they provide, and the the programs' price. A large number of the educators are at ease. They lack the confidence to show others how capable they are of learning new trades and becoming experts in any given talent, therefore they are afraid to venture out and seek out new information.

The majority of these educators also lack the specialized resources required to easily restart their students' learning processes. The rationale behind teachers' dual pursuit of continual learning and traditional instruction is the hat. Most schools will choose to use such corrective actions by attempting to create a setting that is appropriate for the pupils. The corrective actions will also assist the pupils in gaining more of rather than content, the learning resources. Students' ability to conduct research and think critically will benefit them in their ongoing education and help them throughout their lives. Innovative tools that support teachers in teaching through the curriculum are made possible by technology.

Creative teaching tools are beneficial because they present problems to students and teachers and assist them in coming up with solutions.

The process of copying the specifics of the ongoing learning that students do throughout their careers is aided by the addition of innovative materials.

It is critical to create a genuine, workable institutional culture shift. The first action is to attempt to explain to them the importance of learning. It is imperative that you provide a succinct justification for your desire for a cultural shift. Education is much more than just implementing new laws and possibilities.

CHAPTER 8: CONTINUOUS LEARNING DEVELOPMENT

The advantages of mentorship

Any person's fixed attitude and growth mindset can both benefit greatly from learning. The advantages of peer mentoring must be utilized by employees who have a fixed perspective. Peer coaching can be emotionally taxing or even insulting, particularly when the person providing the coaching is someone who may have given up when faced with adversity. You will definitely see a coaching when you have a growth-oriented mindset opportunity as a fantastic chance to advance and get better in the field that closely links to another field.

It is advised that young workers or educators place a high value on a workplace that emphasizes mentoring and role models. A student's career is supported when they have a mentor. It is beneficial to have positive communication with the employee when in such a pleasant setting. An employer's concern for their worker shows the worker that the employer values their contributions and is not merely in it for the money. It is imperative that employers understand how to withhold benefits. anything above and beyond what is required or what you are qualified for in terms of cash remuneration.

People who work in institutions that consciously encourage lifelong learning have been shown to have higher success rates and better salaries. All employees' financial demands have increased, though. Due to their extreme financial hardship, many companies do not feel accountable for their workers' skill development. The self-serving concern that, after five years, a particular person will change careers and work for another company prevents employers from empowering their employees' identities.

Professional development opportunities must also be included into the academic program all year long. It is easier to create and develop this culture through online resources for collaboration and learning. Teachers who are likely graduates already need to find ways to adjust to the changing learning environment. Additionally, they must study continuously and experiment with any new teaching strategies and tools that become available.

Schools and other educational institutions can also support education in all its forms by encouraging faculty and staff to pursue new education, whether in a formal or informal setting. This is just one strategy or action that can be taken to encourage lifelong learning. These can include granting time off for teachers and staff to attend these training sessions, as well as financial assistance if it is available. Teachers who finish their courses can get their tuition reimbursed using available money. A course of study.

Setting annual learning objectives is another use for meeting time for school administrators with staff members. Every teacher receives this treatment. This objective should ideally be something that the instructor or other school staff determines to be a useful learning area. For instance, a teacher may wish to become knowledgeable about the telltale indicators of bullying in high school. The instructor should be encouraged to seize the chance by the school administration. The instructor will be pleased with themselves for achieving this learning objective when it comes time for their evaluation later in the year.

It should be motivating for learners—teachers or staff members who are gaining information—to impart their knowledge to other educators. This can be carried out by the administrators setting up meetings with the teachers. Given that all teachers are interested in this topic, a teacher who completes a course on the global connectedness of schools, for instance, may be requested to discuss what they have learned.

Schools can also support lifelong learning by determining the resources and learning needs of their teachers. It is imperative for administrators to exercise subtlety when gathering this information.

A specific learning opportunity can be communicated to the targeted instructor, together with the support resources available for it.

Another creative approach to implementing continuous learning development—which is characterized by the application of knowledge acquired to benefit society—is to promote learning outside of the workplace. Put differently, learning doesn't always have to occur in a conventional environment, nor does it need to be limited to professional growth. When it affects more than just the classroom and school halls, it is more productive.

We will now quickly discuss how these activities are being evaluated to ascertain their efficacy.

The instructors' post-training knowledge can only be optimal if they are able to use it in the classroom through practice. The specialists and their teams are always researching various models, which demonstrates unequivocally how important it is to have appropriate development models in order to boost the transfer of knowledge through hands-on instruction in a classroom. It is necessary for the development models to incorporate coaching, modeling, practice, and theory. Do development models affect more than just knowledge but also on aptitude and experience? It is important to abandon the traditional understanding of teacher professional development while assessing these programs.

It's best to think of teaching as a technical endeavor requiring both theoretical and practical knowledge. Professional education development can be done in a variety of methods outside of just teaching at a university or other postsecondary institution's classroom. Research in the classroom and scientific laboratory practice are two more ways to learn more about teaching and make informed subject choices. One thing to consider is how frequently children learn science in laboratories. But in order to understand how to instruct scientists, you must sit and communicate with other scientists to learn more. For professional development to be sustainable and contextualized with the appropriate viewpoint, it is essential.

Therefore, it is essential that the entire process of changing education is connected to the work that teachers do and takes place inside the framework of the school programs. It's still not a bad idea to pursue continuous learning, since it continues to be a fundamental requirement in the workforce of the future. As educators advance in their careers, trainers and regulators should come to terms with these realities and develop curricula that provide the most critical resources teachers need to become engaged learners and educators.

The workforce of today desires the freedom to learn in the the background of their regular tasks and have instant access to pertinent training. Many firms are changing the way they organize professional development, feedback, and performance reviews in response to this demand for growth and development.

In the talent competition, training has become a crucial distinction for schools. Opportunities for professional growth included in job descriptions are highly desirable to today's applicant pool. Workers are drawn to organizations that support their employees' success both within and outside of the workplace and place a high importance on lifelong learning. Workers and educators have the opportunity to view their profession

CHAPTER 8: CONTINUOUS LEARNING DEVELOPMENT

through the prism of fresh knowledge or advancements in education. The advancements enable educators to employ fresh, innovative approaches to instruction, resulting in the provision of improved item. The difference that such a breakthrough creates in the standards of a particular institution is the overall benefit.

The most efficient and straightforward ways to improve your writing and reading abilities are covered in the upcoming chapters. In addition to being necessary in all areas of life, these two things can also enhanced. You must read a lot to have a strong vocabulary if you hope to be able to communicate yourself clearly. In addition to teaching you a ton of new vocabulary, this will also teach you how to use them correctly so that you may use them in the most appropriate context when you write. But continuous practice is necessary to become proficient in these skills. If you perform this exercise, it won't be monotonous in the proper manner; this book will teach you everything you need to know.

Yes, writing or composing on your own can be intimidating, but you will find bravery when you finish this book and have the fundamental information needed to begin started. Furthermore, as they say, a man becomes perfect with practice!

9

CHAPTER 9: LEARNING THE BASICS

There are moments when people are confused about writing in English.

This should in no way be disregarded. However, mastering writing techniques takes time. Thus, consistent reading and writing habits are necessary for significant progress in improving your English writing skills.

Let's talk about writing abilities. Be sure there are no basic spelling, grammatical, or punctuation errors when you rapidly go over your primary English skills in preparation for your job application portfolio. You may simply prevent simple mistakes by proofreading your content. The quality of your English writing on your job application will determine whether you are selected for an interview or not.

Learn and Master

To learn English, you must first work on your grammar. Simply put, grammar is the arrangement of words in a sentence to convey the meaning of what you want to say. When you attempt to create a lengthy sentence or utilize terms for which you are unsure of their exact meaning, you run the risk of making grammar errors. Hence, until you gain proficiency, it is best to compose brief sentences using basic grammar structures.

The spelling of words is the second thing you should be aware of. If you are unsure of how to spell a term, you should use one of the many online spell checkers. To make sure you are writing correctly, you should also be careful to adjust the spellchecker tool to "UK English" or "US English" depending on the situation.

Punctuation is the third item that is consistently disregarded. Common mistakes include not using commas to divide lists of items, using an apostrophe instead of an inverted comma when quoting someone, and more. If you don't take care of it, just putting the words in the right order won't make sense.

Your ability to learn English through reading will determine the basis of your English writing skill improvement. Has this ever been how you felt? Let's say you've read something in the papers. If someone asked you what you had read in the newspaper 30 minutes later, you couldn't Recall it. It is not because you forgot what you had read that accounts for your inability to recall the information. The explanation behind this is because you were reading the newspaper passively rather than actively. Therefore, you should actively read in order to retain the information and pick up new skills that will help you write in English.

CHAPTER 9: LEARNING THE BASICS

As you actively read anything, you can underline important terms to help you remember them, sum up the main ideas, pose questions, and research related information. You will find that these key exercises greatly assist you in expressing your opinions about the material you have studied.

Gearing Up Your Brain to Read Faster

Reading to learn English is a useful tool for everyone. Everyone is living in a world that moves quickly these days. Nowadays, information serves as the basis for every choice.

You must therefore read everything more quickly than ever, from emails to paperwork to reports. The key to solving these issues is speed reading.

This article will teach you four strategies to prime your brain to develop rapid reading habits.

Discover the Skipping Art: Did you know that the human brain can comprehend a topic's fundamental idea without reading between the lines? If you have ever read any non-fiction books, you will be familiar with its format. You read the book's introduction through and learn it by heart first. Next, pay attention to the subtitles and subheads. Read the subheadings' initial few lines as well as their final line. At least forty percent of the key knowledge in the book will be retained by you. With this method, reading will go more quickly than before.

Control Your Mind: Regulate your ideas when you read a topic. To help your brain recognize the important issue, concentrate on it.

Make a connection with the precise phrases that have a connection to real-world experience. For instance, consider the tension you have experienced in your life if you read about stress management. In this manner, you may readily relate to the subject and retain it in your mind.

Avoid Subvocalizing When Reading: Mouthing what they read is a terrible habit for certain people. Studies reveal that speaking softly slows down of reading. Stop such a habit right away if you have one. Carefully read, make note of the keywords, and then move on to the next section.

Establish a Target to Gather the Vital Data: Why are you reading about a certain topic? Ask yourself. Let's say you are reading a book about physical activity. Concentrate on your fitness objective.

Choose those sections of the book to help you reach your objective. Go over fitness-related aspects and compile the knowledge that will help you.

How Does the Brain Work When You Read Fast?

It's interesting to note that your brain saves the image and comprehends everything as soon as you see the words when reading. Numerous studies conducted between 1868 and the present have demonstrated that reading is solely a mental function and is unrelated to subvocalization. Consequently, you need to practice reading aloud without using subtitles if you want to read more quickly.

Rather than reading every word, you might make it a habit to read a few words at a time. This will enable you to read more quickly.

Normal reading and the brain

You utilize your tongue and lips to read and speak the words, your ear to hear what you read, your eyes to view the words, and your brain to analyze the words' semantics when you read something. Even if you don't read aloud, you still read and speak the words in your head.

Hence, subvocalization is a reading habit that you have had since you were a little child. Thus, your brain typically performs the following tasks when you read anything:

Process Visual Information: Words represent the information your eyes view when you read. The pictures register in your brain, and it begins processing them. Every word is processed, recognized, and stored in the memory zone.

Process Acoustic Information: The words you read are also stored as acoustic information in a specific language in the memory of your brain. This means that your brain stores the visual representations of the words into acoustic information when you hear or read something using your mouth and tongue.

Process Semantic Information: Using language you are familiar with, the brain examines both visual and aural data to determine the relationship meaning between the two messages. Then you comprehend the significance of what As you read.

The above three phases take time for the brain to absorb, which makes it difficult to read quickly during the typical reading process.

Processing of Visual Information

Your brain records the visual information of words whenever you see something while reading, and it then processes that information. In other words, visual information processing refers to your brain's capacity to interpret and evaluate visual stimuli. Your brain analyzes the information and stores it in your memory so you can access it later. Your brain's capacity to digest information determines how quickly you can analyze the data. How quickly and precisely you can engage with the system depends on how strong your brain is. conditions and surroundings to which you are subjected. Thus, in a nutshell, visual information processing means that you can feel, interpret, and comprehend what you are seeing because of general cognition, developed perception, and other brain activity.

information processing that gives your eyes the ability to quickly and automatically identify what they see. The eyes typically focus on a word or object for a quarter to a third of a second before moving on to the next one. Your eyes go back to the object and reread it in order for your brain to identify the name of the object or word that your eyes have seen. The term keeps coming up in your vision until your brain acknowledges it.

If you suffer from any visual problems, such as binocular instability or eye tracking disorder, you might not be able to process the information.

In those situations, you require medical attention and supervision.

Factors Restricting the Brain's Speed Capability Perusing

The same things that make it harder for your brain to comprehend visual information quickly also make it harder for your brain to read quickly. Below is a discussion of those:

Saccade: Your eyes are not at rest when you read; your body may be at rest and your head may be concentrated on the words you are reading with intense concentration. You will notice that these are gazing at the words if you try to sense what your eyes are doing. This Your eyes move in a jerky motion known as saccade. Two visual degrees make up each saccade, which can often hold eight letters at once. Every saccade in the eyes is completed in a mere .3 seconds.

Fixation: Your eyes fixate on words for three milliseconds while you read. You do not shift your eyes between the saccades in that split second. Put otherwise, if a page has ten lines and each word has an average of five letters, it could take your eyes four seconds to read a line.

Acoustical Processing: Your brain's acoustical processing causes your reading to slow down. Acquiring the words, encoding the data, keeping it in memory, and retrieving it are all parts of acoustic processing. the data from memory through reencoding. These are the fundamental components of your brain's auditory system at work while you read the text. As a result, mouthing or articulating words causes your eyes to scan across them more slowly.

Subvocalization: When reading, your voice cords are used. Even some individuals read aloud. You hear the words in your ears as well as pronounce them in your head when you read. It's called subvocalization. Your reading speed naturally decreases when you have to listen to the words that you see and read, which is not necessary.

How to Overcome these Limiting Barriers to Speed Reading?

The world is moving so quickly these days that you have to read more than ever in order to do your task. Thus, reading more quickly is necessary at this point in time. While you might need to read 600–800 words per minute, the average person can read 150–250 words per minute. How are you going to accomplish that?

You'll learn several strategies for breaking down hurdles to quick reading here.

When reading, guide your eyes with your finger: Using your finger to guide your eyes to the text you are reading is a novel method of starting to read. By doing this, you can reduce sub-vocalization and train your brain to pick up clusters of words rather than reading each one individually.

Put Your Mouth Away and Tongue to Pronounce Words: Talk

to your brain instead of focusing on how you pronounce the words. For example, you could stop chewing gum in your mouth while reading in order to break your previous habit. This will reduce the need of subvocalization.

Play Some Music While Reading: While reading, listening to music can be therapeutic. It lowers your sub-vocalization while simultaneously improving your reading attention.

It's been observed that classical music is more effective at minimizing subvocalization.

Utilize the RSVP app: You can increase your reading speed by using software designed for speed reading, which reduces sub-vocalization. These programs are straightforward and simple to use. These apps accelerate your reading speed with Rapid Serial Visual Presentation. All you have to do is can copy a paragraph into the application's textbox and adjust the word count that is spoken out loud each minute. It is advised to start reading at a pace of at least 300 words per minute in order to form a habit. The reduction of your subvocalization and your ability to increase the speed at which you read will amaze you.

Develop Your Brain's Skim and Scan Skills

The term "scanning" describes a reading strategy that can help you understand the key concepts of the material you are reading. Scanning assists you in discover the essential details to respond to the query posed by the subject. Let's say you are reading a trip book. By scanning a book, you can help your brain remember important details such as how many locations of various interests are there.

The process of comprehending an idea's fundamental idea is known as skimming. When reading a nonfiction topic, the skimming strategy is useful. It's similar to looking over a city map and tracking the locations that catch your attention with your digit. Your brain acquires additional information required for travel, such as the location of the destinations you want to visit, the closest hotels, landmarks, markets, and communication data. By doing this, you can teach your brain to comprehend and retain the information you read for extended periods of time.

The definition of preview in the dictionary is the capacity to view something before it is publicly available. In other words, previewing is a method of gathering all relevant data that could be discovered via skimming and scanning methods. In addition, Preview provides responses to the five WH questions—who, what, when, where, and why. "Who" denotes the individual, "what" denotes the subject, "when" indicates the moment, "where" denotes the location, and "why" provides information. regarding the causes. In other words, preview helps your brain gather all the necessary data for skimming and scanning.

Advantages of Scanning and Skimming

Principal Concepts: The capacity to understand the underlying ideas that have been stated in a book is the biggest advantage of using skimming and scanning strategies when reading it.

Increase Knowledge: Skimming a book can help you learn a lot more without getting into the specifics.

How? Start by examining the book's layout, which includes a table of contents, chapter summaries, excerpt boxes, and other features. A quick glance at these contents will assist you in broadening your core understanding.

Proficiency with Books as a Tool: A proficient reader is able to determine the how to organize a book's main reading subjects to improve learning outcomes. This strategy will help you gain confidence in your ability to read or skip a book. If reading is required, your experience will indicate how much more in-depth analysis is required to fully understand the book's content.

Tempo: To increase reading speed, skimming and scanning techniques are applied. To get more knowledge from your everyday routine and learn more, you should utilize the strategy as a tool to obtain new knowledge.

Techniques for Skimming and Scanning

You can practice scanning and skimming by following the methods listed below:

- Examine the title of the text
- Check out the contents table.
- Examine the details on the book's rear cover page.
- Examine the index.
- Go over each chapter's name.
- Examine the headlines
- Read the paragraphs' first two or three sentences.
- Take a look at the bolded text.
- Examine the pictures

CHAPTER 9: LEARNING THE BASICS

- Graphs and spot tables
- Include a synopsis and conclusion for each chapter.
- Jot down the essential details.

Read Quickly sweeping

As you are aware, skimming is the procedure used on dairy farms to skim the cream from the top of the milk. The most significant part of the milk is the cream. This also holds true for distilling the most important details from a subject. Finding the essential information and the primary idea in a book without delving into every detail of the subject is crucially, the primary goal of skimming when reading quickly. You can skip other unnecessary information and use the book to obtain the information you require. Put another way, it's not as vital to read quickly as it is to skim in order to filter out or sift through the unimportant content and concentrate on what matters most.

Prior to quickly scanning the main points of a subject, you need know when it's appropriate to skim. In real life, skimming could be beneficial in the following scenarios:

It goes without saying that a complex and long business report may be the ideal subject for skimming.

By using short words to grab readers' attention, news editors create content that is visually appealing.

When you're short on time and have to If you read a lot of content, your best bet will be to skim.

It is usually advised, therefore, to read the entire paragraph, including the outline and conclusion, as these are where the writer presents their objective opinions or the topic's foundation and wraps up by summarizing their observations and research.

The Predisposition to Skim Before Reading

Skimming is a useful tool that can be applied in challenging circumstances; it is not a usual course of life. You must therefore adjust to it. Before you can adjust to it, you must practice a lot. Prior to starting the exercise, you should be aware of various skimming hints and techniques.

What Should Be Noted While Previewing: A helpful starting point for your journey of skimming and aiming is prereading. to stay away from the pointless reading content included in books.

By prereading a book, you may determine which sections you already know and which ones you still need to read to improve your understanding. Prereading, then, is planning a reading strategy to finish a book quickly. The prereading technique entails looking at and considering the chapter titles, headings and subheadings, summaries, and conclusions of the chapters as well as reviewing and responding to the questions at the end of each chapter. Prereading also aims to improve your vocabulary, help you develop concepts, and improve your reading speed.

Recognize Your Prereading Goals: Each and every action has a goal. Consider a sportsperson. A sportsperson gets their body warmed up. before to engaging in the sport. In addition to getting the athlete's body ready, the warm-up helps them focus their attention entirely on their sport. This also applies to your prereading time. It helps you choose the important subjects you should read, and it also gets your mind ready to focus on and learn new information rapidly.

It also significantly increases your comprehension of the subject and aids in helping you visualize what you want to read. Thus, the primary goal of prereading is to incorporate new concepts into the already-formed mental framework of the main topic.

The Four Ps of Prereading: Preview, Predict, Previous knowledge, and The four Ps of prereading are purpose.

Before you begin reading the book, the preview helps you gain a general understanding of its contents.

Anticipating aids in selecting the important section of the book to read in order to understand the new ideas that are expounded upon within.

Your desire to learn about the new concepts presented in the book is greatly heightened if you are familiar with its contents.

The goal you achieved by expanding on your past knowledge while reading the book is the purpose.

Pose Queries: Understanding the rationale for prereading causes your mind to submit certain queries regarding the novel ideas covered in the book before you begin prereading. Thus, simply observing the extra material presented in the book, your mind begins to wonder. It happens naturally. This occurs not because you are looking at new information, but rather because you already know a little bit about the subject and may have certain questions that you are unable to find the answers to. Therefore, it is best to make a list of the questions before beginning the prereading. Your prereading will have served its objective if you do this.

Use guides to practice speed reading.

Rapid Serial Visual Presentation (RSVP) software is a useful tool for accelerating speed reading, as this chapter has already covered. You can learn more about some of these programs here, which can be an enjoyable method to improve your speed reading abilities.

Word Processor: It's an app that works with the Kindle that facilitates rapid reading. To assist you in reading it word by word, the software shows each line, word by word. Through the settings option, you can adjust the speed at which the words appear on the screen. To get used to the procedure, you can initially vary the speed from 50 words per minute to 250 words per minute based on your typical reading speed. Next, adjust the pace to enhance your reading speed. The typical reading speed of an individual is 250 words per minute. If you practice regularly, you can even read 900 words per minute. But if needed, there are other alternatives to halt and go back in time.

Spreeder It's a free internet application. Additionally, you Make use of this app when you're speed reading. You must paste the text you wish to practice speed reading here. The texts are shown word for word for your practice here, just like they are in Word Runner.

"Reading quickly is the best!" It's the name of the software application. You may get the app from the Google Play Store and the Apple App Store. Compared to the other two applications mentioned above, this one is a little different. It doesn't include a text field where you could paste stuff to read faster. Rather, it provides a number of exercises that will genuinely improve your speed reading skills. These drills involve looking up words in a text, looking up numbers to memorize, etc. These exercises improve your ability to focus your thoughts. increase your capacity for concentration, sharpen your memory, and read more quickly.

Unlearning Your Practice Reading Strategies in Elementary School

Without a doubt, you started reading in your early years, just like everyone else. You had done as your teacher had instructed in phonics. Phonics aids in the correspondence between sound and letter and symbol in the alphabet. Thus, phonics is a teaching strategy to help kids practice reading. Despite this, comprehension is another part of reading that is just as vital as phonics.

The most regrettable development is that studies trying to determine how effective school-based teachers are at teaching phonics to students and connecting phonics to comprehension have discovered a highly frustrating and erroneous state of affairs. It suggests that educators lack the necessary training to help kids develop their comprehension skills.

You might be one of those people who struggles with understanding, which could cause you to read more slowly. Perhaps this is the reason why your reading pace is decreasing.

In a 2001 report, the US government's National Reading Panel (NRP) recommended five "pillars" of education for improving reading skills. Phonics, phonemic awareness, fluency, vocabulary, and improving comprehension are some of these pillars. Vocabulary, the fourth pillar, improves your ability to comprehend during a speed reading session.

Therefore, all you need to do before beginning your speed-reading session is to forget or unlearn the methods your early reading instruction taught you.

Using any of the previously mentioned speed-reading applications, you ought to prioritize the speed first. Next, you ought to focus on expanding your vocabulary.

Every time you come across a new word, stop reading quickly and record it in your notebook along with its definition. Understand the word's phonics to help your memory recall it correctly. Restart your speed reading.

Nothing occurs instantly. Therefore, it may take a varied amount of time for each person to reach the necessary level of speed reading. You might even need to read the same material for a week or longer in order to improve your vocabulary, phonics, and comprehension. You will notice that as you practice consistently on a new subject, your comprehension and speed reading abilities have improved and you are outperforming yourself.

10

CHAPTER 10: READING SPEED

Instead of reading every word on a page, speed reading is the practice of quickly grasping and identifying phrases and understanding sentences. More information than ever before is continuously available to you from the world around you. The majority of individuals can read 250 words per minute on average. Even Nevertheless, there are certain individuals there whose natural reading speed is higher than others'. By using speed reading techniques, you might increase your reading speed by at least two times. You will learn how to read faster in this section.

Techniques for Rapid Reading

Do you have a reading habit where you move your finger under the text in your reading materials? It's possible that your childhood teacher taught you this method of reading in the hopes that your Concentrating on reading could improve your ability to comprehend. No, not at all. It doesn't improve your comprehension skills or help you concentrate when reading. On the other hand, rapid reading is hindered when one places a finger beneath each line while reading. You are forced to go slowly by the crutch of the finger under the line. In light of this, it is highly recommended that you refrain from using your finger during your reading exercise going forward while discussing speed reading approaches.

Turning pages slowly is the second bad habit that prevents people from reading at a fast pace. It's also possible that you've noticed that, unlike when you move a page in your reading, your thought process never stops. A quick reader reads a lengthy paragraph in 4-5 seconds, but the ordinary reader takes 4-5 seconds or longer to turn a page and stops reading at the conclusion. Thus, it affects you in two ways if you take a long time to turn a page. To begin with, it takes longer to read, and to make up for the time it takes to flip the page, it diverts your attention. So, the moment the page-turning problem becomes a problem, adjust your reading habit quickly. It is best to open the book and hold it with both hands when reading, as opposed to putting your finger under the line. Next, grab ten to fifteen pages at a time, hold them in your right hand, read them, and turn them swiftly the page with your left hand when you finish reading it. This will maintain the same pace for your reading and thinking.

Skimmimg: When you skim content while reading, you do so consciously in order to obtain a clear picture of the content you find most interesting.

Consequently, skimming serves a few distinct functions.

It seeks to extract the theoretical underpinnings from the extensive reading list.

It assists you in removing the pointless sections from the reading content.

It securely displays the key points that you need to focus on and read carefully.

It enables you to locate the article's main material from a high perspective without having to understand every little element.

That being said, you should use caution when choosing to forego reading content. The choice-based reading articles listed below are appropriate for skimming:

Periodicals

Books that are not fiction

websites, manuals, etc.

With one notable exception, skimming is fairly similar to previewing. The one exception is if you skim and read the first two or three sentences rather than just one. After then, you swivel your gaze to look for the keywords throughout the passage. In addition, you look for names, dates, numbers, and any other relevant information that might be particularly significant to you. In order to quickly understand the same, you read the paragraph's final sentence.

Examining It functions in opposition to skimming. Just consider the activity you perform when working on the following tasks; it is known as scanning in formal terminology.

Sorted alphabetically phone book entries with phone numbers indexed for each name.

A book should have an index at the back and a table of contents at the front.

sports scoreboard.

TV schedules.

investigating a subject or piece of content online.

By the way, scanning and skimming can complement one other. You may have quickly skimmed the newspaper's news headlines and then quickly perused the article, perhaps looking for more detailed information to pay attention to.

Ignoring: You should practice skipping in addition to using skimming and scanning when reading an article, as failing to do so will force you to read through the pointless content.

You will be able to skip that section of the paragraph when your speed reading skills improve because it is completely useless to you. Therefore, skipping is advantageous in the following situations: A certain segment of the reading material contains nothing new or significant. Nothing that could be helpful to you is covered.

Ways to Boost Up Your Reading Speeds

It's time to go over ways to increase your reading speed now. You can find eight tried-and-true methods to get better at reading here.

Put an end to the monologue: The inner monologue, also known as subvocalization, is a widespread occurrence that almost everyone experiences. Monologue or subvocalization is the process of mouthing the words aloud or softly through the vocal cord, perceiving the sound in the ears, and sending the sound to the brain. Your reading pace will mostly decrease as a result of this event. Now that you are an adult and can comprehend the meaning of a word by simply looking at it, you should simply look at the words and process them mentally rather than mouthing them. You can quit mouthing things. Listen to relaxing music with a headset.

Word-chunking: Rather than reading each word aloud, you start reading a few words at a time when you are practicing stopping the monologue. This stage aims to teach your brain and sight to function in tandem so that your brain can analyze a group of words and comprehend their meaning without the need for subvocalization. One of the most effective strategies to quicken your reading is word chunking.

It's important to keep in mind that word chunking and halting the monologue together can significantly increase your reading speed.

Avoid Reread: You will notice that your eyes are jumping and darting when you read if you pay close attention to someone or even yourself. on the text. It indicates that the eyes are not moving back and forth across the text in an even or fluid manner, which is ideal for fast reading. It's a cunning habit that develops quickly. The method to prevent it, though it may seem a little juvenile, is to move forward and never turn back when oscillating your finger across a page.

Use Your Side Vision If you can successfully complete the first three steps in a succession, your reading habit will improve significantly. You'll see that you've been able to fixate your gaze on the line's middle and see the entire thing. We refer to this as peripheral vision. Once you start reading a line using this method, you take it in with your peripheral vision and mentally process it, you'll be one step closer to reaching your speed reading objective.

Set a timer: Now is the moment to take an exam to see if your speed reading has increased. Put a timer on, say, for one minute. When the allotted time has elapsed, begin reading as usual and stop. Count how many pages you have read so far. Continue to practice each day. Establish a weekly target for yourself and always aim to beat your previous best time. You can practice speed reading until you achieve the desired result.

Boost Your Word Power: Are you having trouble gaining speed during your practice runs because of your inadequate vocabulary? Do you pause to learn the meaning of a word or do you pass over it? In fact, you are considerably slowing down your speed-reading process when you choose to handle an unfamiliar word in any way. Therefore, you must expand your vocabulary by learning new terms in order to work on strengthening it.

Your reading variety will expand with time, and you'll start to notice that you're reading books more quickly than you used to.

Your self-assurance will soar, and you'll decide to establish a new objective for yourself: reading quickly.

Continue Reading: The saying "practice makes perfect" is timeless. Consider the experts in their fields, such as those in medicine, law, painting, music, etc. They routinely practice. and reach the pinnacle of excellence. Regular practice of speed reading is also recommended. Your level of perfection will increase with your reading proficiency.

Examine the Key Points: Not to mention, practice skimming.

Grab a book that you enjoy reading. Read the table of contents first, followed by the captions for the diagrams, the subtitles, etc. After that, start reading each chapter's and section's opening paragraph. Read the conclusion of each chapter as well. Now close your eyes, take a few deep breaths, and let yourself cool. Bring what you've read together in your thoughts. Next, reread the book using the approach that has been covered thus far, taking everything into consideration. You will discover that you have read more of the book. quickly and much more effectively than before understood the reading content.

Determine Your Reading Main Focus

Throughout your academic career, you may have encountered the question, "What was the main idea?" after reading a paragraph. After reading a passage or paragraph for a comprehension test, this was a fairly typical scenario. Answering the passage's questions frequently seemed challenging to several students, not because they hadn't read the piece but rather because they hadn't grasped its main premise.

Thus, learning the reading skill is necessary to comprehend the main idea of a paragraph as well as other linked issues like the author's perspective, expressing your own opinion, building vocabulary, etc. You will find techniques here. to determine the primary theme or subject of your reading.

Define the primary Idea: You must comprehend the inner meaning of the primary idea before you can concentrate on it. A passage's primary idea is the author's principal notion, around which the passage has been based. A sentence is considered a topic sentence if it summarizes the author's major point in one line. The paragraph's overall structure is established by that sentence, which also discusses the topic of the paragraph.

In the lines that follow the paragraph's topic sentence, the author provides details that support the main point. This is the kind of topic you would find in an essay. In this instance The main idea of a thesis, or multi-paragraph topic, is found in a distinct section called the thesis statement. The thesis statement, or core idea, is covered in full in a thesis.

Nevertheless, the major idea's opening line briefly discusses the core theme without delving into detail.

The following paragraphs or sentences that describe more specifics and add nuances go into greater detail about the main theme.

One article that addresses the rationale behind digital marketing's superiority over traditional marketing in the twenty-first century, for example, might come to mind. There is a paragraph at the start of the topic that may detail the customer's experiences in completing the At the close of the 20th century, consumers' perceptions of traditional marketing were declining, and they were being exposed to emerging digital marketing as a substitute. It is the author's duty to outline the arguments' structural framework at the outset and then develop the ideas in the paragraphs that follow by examining additional topics and subtleties.

It is implied that the major notion is ingrained in the issue when the author does not state it explicitly. In that instance, it is your duty as a reader to seek for keywords that the author uses frequently and to analyze the figures, pictures, graphs, diagrams, and other visual aids in order to determine the main point the author is trying to make.

Locate the primary Idea: A few particular pointers are provided below to assist you in pinpointing the primary idea.

Determine the Topic: Carefully read the paragraph and make an effort to ascertain what it is trying to say. Don't go overboard trying to figure out the reasoning behind the major idea's framing.

After carefully reading the material, summarize it in one sentence using your own words. Inform someone about the topic of the paragraph and get their opinion. Compare it to what you know.

Attention to the First and Last Sentences Pay close attention to the opening and closing phrases of the paragraph since these may contain the author's hint about the major theme. Observe whether the writer has utilized.

Eliminate All Diversions The practice of reading is a brain-nourishing art. The body and mind must give the brain its complete attention in order to nourish it. You may already be aware of how sensitive brain cells are to both the body and the mind. For this reason, failing to pay even a minimal attention to detail could prevent you from reading and understanding. Here are some essential reading strategies that will force you to read the material with complete focus even if you have little or no interest in it.

Turn off every messaging device. Currently, you are in a very challenging scenario where you have little to no control over the instant messages that appear on your devices. The alert sound of the messages are the most annoying and attention-grabbing thing to happen on a regular basis. Even a single gentle beep can disrupt your reading and take your attention away from the subject at hand when you are creating mental models in your head to understand the context of what you are reading. Therefore, it's a good idea to turn off any electronics that can divert your attention.

Establish a reading atmosphere: Setting up the ideal space for reading is the first step toward developing a solid reading habit.

What is the ideal reading environment, one would wonder? First, clear out all clutter, human movement, and reminders of other tasks from any lonely spots in your house. Second, put on earbuds and listen to music to prevent background noise. Play some calming instrumental music and focus entirely on reading. Thirdly, make sure you're well satisfied so that nothing will be able to divert your focus from reading, like hunger or thirst.

Make Reading Entertaining When you read something, you

might not agree with its substance or find the writing style or language standard objectionable. Reading about such a subject might tire you. Therefore, in order to avoid reading about a dull subject, you might ask your virtual friend Google to look up some academic papers, online lectures, or YouTube tutorials on the subject. These resources may pique your interest and help you find the pertinent information you need.

Examine the Reading List: Examine the book briefly before beginning to read. Look for any is any heading or lists that you may find interesting that the author mentioned. The author brings up such topics to grab the reader's attention right away and let them know that the topic they are searching for has already been covered in the book.

Make a "Read and Recall" plan. Practice Reading: Regression occurs when readers are made to read something they don't particularly want to read about. This results from a strong interest in the subject. It takes longer with this practice to understand the main idea of the subject. Making it a practice to read one paragraph at a time, close your eyes, and reflect on what you learnt from it is one technique to solve this kind of issue. Recognize the primary concept of that paragraph and summarize it in one or two phrases. Continue using the same strategy when you read the following paragraphs.

Embrace Reading with a Study-Buddy Perspective: Listening has a greater learning impact than reading. Understanding, even a dry subject, may become more engaging if you hear it from someone else rather than reading about it yourself. Treating a friend who has a good outlook on the same subject can foster an atmosphere that could make the material easier for you to understand. It could be a lot of pleasure to understand the unresolved concerns through hearing.

Have Fun While Reading: Energy levels are always raised by having a playful mentality. A person's level of comprehension and degree of conceptualization determine how quickly they can read a page. of focus on the subject.

Remember when you were a kid and everything was meant to be a game? Relive the good old days. Read the same material again, but this time, set a timer to alert you when it's time to finish. Read the passage again while attempting to beat your prior time record. It will encourage you to read more quickly.

Adopt Good Sitting Posture: One of the main causes of overstress when working while seated for extended periods of time is poor sitting posture. As you read, your level of mental stress keeps rising. Therefore, avoid putting additional strain on your body from incorrect sitting posture. Select a chair with a backrest so that you can read comfortably, and Maintain a flat foot strike on the ground.

Before reading, practice meditation. It's common knowledge that meditation helps you focus better on reading and other tasks while also revitalizing your spirit. Thus, it is recommended that you meditate for one or two minutes before beginning to read. This will help you clear your thoughts and focus more intently on what you are reading.

Set Aside Time Every 50 Minutes: Have you ever had a lesson at your school, college, or university last more than fifty minutes? If your response is "No," the next inquiry is: "Why?" Research has shown that the human brain can focus its entire attention on a subject for up to 50 minutes at a time. The level of attentiveness declines after that.

Thus, you ought to take a Ten minutes should be taken off after every fifty minutes of reading so that you can focus and replenish your energy.

Do Some Warm-Up

To complete any task, a strategy is required. Before a test, a student needs to study extensively. Athletes must have a solid workout regimen before engaging in their sport. Every motion must be practiced by an actor prior to putting on the play on stage. So, a warm-up is necessary before any action.

The situation with a reader is similar. Activating the reader's brain is part of their warm-up. However, it's not always a difficult task to read a book. However, there are several prereading exercises that could spice up your reading.

Pre-Reading Assignments

The primary factor that determines how much reading you can do and how interested you can get in it is motivation. Getting some prior knowledge on the subject is one approach to read the material and become interested in it. understanding of the book.

Assemble Prior Knowledge: Reading any kind of non-fictional material, such as a book, journal, scholarly article, report, or other, can be beneficial if you are aware of the reason behind it beforehand. Therefore, it is crucial to establish your goals and understand why you are reading.

Examine the chapters and select the ideas that you believe are most important.

Consider the reading materials from the perspective of a learner to determine what you need to establish a strong conceptual foundation.

Think about the chapter's troubleshooting section.

Take note of the chapter's valuable resources, which include questions, learning objectives, glossaries, margin notes, and chapter summaries.

While Reading Activities You become aware of the goal of your reading during the pre-reading activity. Reading is a task. that broadens the knowledge base you already possess.

Acquire Information: Thus, as you read, you should take targeted action. Building a bridge between "What is new to you?" and "What is known to you?" is your aim while reading.

While reading, go over what you have already learnt.

Consider, for example, that you are reading a chapter on "US Business under Global Perspective." Ask yourself, "What do you already know?" Remember what you learned in the last chapter.

Do you know if a US company has international operations?

What issues do you think the US company might have had with its international operations?

Boost Your Fluency in Reading

Sometimes reading fluency can affect your ability to understand what you are reading. Reading fluency and context comprehension are essential while reading. run at the same speed in parallel. You must read the same sentence again in order to grasp it if your memory requires longer time to interpret the text and the decoding speed does not match your reading pace. It's possible to become sidetracked from your reading in such a difficult environment. Here are some tips for improving your reading fluency.

Record reading and read aloud: Reading something aloud and recording it for subsequent listening could be one method to increase your reading fluency. You will comprehend how you have been reading, when you have been halting, when you have been taking longer to read, etc., when you listen to the tape.

Additionally, hearing aids in be quicker to encode and decode the material, simplifying and enjoying the learning process. You can use this to assess and enhance your reading fluency and style.

Utilize a ruler or your finger to follow the sentence: To start, you can move along the phrase with your finger, a pencil, or a ruler to increase your reading fluency and prevent distractions. Maintaining focus on the sentences on a page requires a lot of attention. Actually, when you move the pencil along the phrase with your finger, your eye follows suit, reading the entire line at the same speed. Throughout the drill, if you quicken the forward motion of your finger with your eyes will likewise move more quickly than they did previously. You can increase your reading fluency in this method.

Read the Same Subject Multiple Times: You will become more proficient if you practice more. It is necessary to read the same material multiple times, especially if you want to improve your reading abilities. Repeatedly reading about the same subject develops fluency. Reading aloud repeatedly exposes your brain to the same words and sentences. As a result, you'll realize that reading is becoming lot easier every time. You'll feel more motivated and appreciate yourself for it. Additionally, you'll improve your comprehension abilities and learn contextual cues from the information much more quickly as a result of this.

Developing Pre-Reading Vocabulary: It might be entirely normal that reading a fresh article could introduce you to some new words. Therefore, it would be beneficial to make an effort to learn as many new terms as you can from the article you have selected to read. Jot down the new terms that have acceptable meanings in your vocabulary. Important new terms are included in the table of contents, index, glossary, and chapter headers.

By building up your vocabulary before reading an article, you'll be able to read faster and retain the content better.

Make Use of a Range of Books for Various Interests: It is possible that you are not finding the book you have selected to read fluently to be all that engaging. It may occur if you sense the background of The book is uninteresting. As a result of being forced to develop reading fluency with such a dull subject, you experience excitement and annoyance rather than passion for reading. Give up trying to practice fluency with a book like that that doesn't interest you.

Pick a variety of books from your selection of choices, such as detective stories, poetry, comic books, etc. Start by reading little pieces of writing at first, and then progressively expand your reading to include longer stories. Over time, this will also help you become more patient when reading. With your best books, you'll feel at ease and be able to read more fluently faster.

Establish a Stress-Free Environment: Anxiety and stress are two typical foes that prevent your mind from focusing on quality reading. reading with ease at huge, need a tranquil setting. Select your optimal time when there won't be a deadline for any other task, your body will be completely energized, and your mind will be stress-free. You will be able to concentrate entirely on improving your reading fluency in such a setting.

11

CHAPTER 11: VISUALIZATION AND CONCEPTUALIZATION

Developing mental imagery through visualization is a powerful tool that can enhance both your learning and performance. It is normal for daydreaming, memory, and imagination to be accompanied by visual imagery. However, some people find it challenging to evoke these kinds of vivid pictures. They thus experience difficulty learning new things or doing any kind of task. The term "congenital aphantasia" is currently used to describe the incapacity to conjure up mental images. The foundations of literacy are reading comprehension and word meaning acquisition, both of which depend heavily on mental picture.

Dual-coding theory was introduced by Allan Paivio of the University of Western Ontario in 1971. It clarifies that the most fundamental form of nonverbal representation is mental imagery. Another type of mental process is verbal. Both orally and visually are two distinct methods for information storage. These two codes can be used separately or in combination to improve learning and memory abilities.

CHAPTER 11: VISUALIZATION AND CONCEPTUALIZATION

Understanding concepts of abstract objects can be aided by mental imagery. Mind maps are a useful tool for organizing and remembering knowledge. Questionnaires are used by the researchers to gauge how vivid people's mental images are. An individual's score on this exam will be used to correlate the amount of activity measured in the brain's vision region. Measuring the variations in a person's vivid mental image can be useful in identifying those who suffer from aphantasia.

Reading quickly stimulates the sense of sight.

Louis Emile Javal, a French ophthalmologist from the late 19th century, clarified that ocular Reading movement makes use of visuals related to the written context. He said that the eyes move quickly and in brief bursts, alternating with fixations and avoiding a continuous path along a text line.

Three significant changes occurred in the middle of the 20th century: first, non-invasive eye movement tracking equipment became more advanced; second, computer technology was established, which facilitated the faster collection and storage of records and processing of large amounts of eye movement data; and third, cognitive psychology was brought in to strengthen the theoretical and methodological foundations of reading instruction.

CHAPTER 11: VISUALIZATION AND CONCEPTUALIZATION

How Can I Visualize Effectively?

Visualization exercises improve reading comprehension abilities to gain a deeper comprehension of the material, which and an Someone uses the words to conjure up images in their mind while they read carefully. When someone intentionally trains this skill, they can immediately picture the text. They can have a positive reading experience and retain the information they have read since they can envision while they are reading. An individual can identify with a text when they visualize it while reading or hearing it. Storybook readers, for instance, are able to immerse themselves in the narrative by imagining the characters. It facilitates their understanding of the significance of reading and motivates them to keep reading that book.

To begin practicing visualization, pick a passage that has a lot of strong verbs. and languages that are descriptive. You can begin at any point that will enable you to visualize the scene clearly. It is not necessary to start reading a book from cover to cover. You might choose a concise paragraph or a well-organized sentence to learn how to visualize. The following are some ways that you can use to visualize successfully.

Reading: You can work on your ability to visualize by reading aloud on your own, listening to a text, or participating in small group reading exercises. You can urge yourself to envision more by turning out the lights and closing your eyes while you listen.

If you read aloud to a small group of people, you can stop regularly to exchange mental pictures. The textbook is a crucial tool in strengthening your capacity to produce visual imagery. Using a textbook with fewer graphics or one without is beneficial. A proficient textbook writer use descriptive language to aid readers in creating their own mental imagery.

Writing: Strong verbs and descriptive language are important tools for evoking vivid images in the minds of young writers, and it is imperative that we support them in using them. Your writing and idea-crafting processes are influenced by the visuals in your mind. It enables you to approach a book or narrative with fresh thoughts, scenarios, and plots.

Availability: Your mind is capable of conjuring up a mental picture involving the previously stored items. Effective visualization requires that you expose yourself to going through many experiences. It will be necessary for you to read books, view movies, and engage in other activities. It will support the development of realistic and intricate mental imagery. Your awareness and understanding will yield more information or facts to your thoughts when you visualize something in your head.

Enhancing Visualization Skills

Experts in physiology have clarified that a person's sensory input is crucial to strong and healthy visualization. Additionally, the visuals are necessary for memory retention in an individual. Visualizing the action you initially performed can activate your nerve system and convey a message to your brain about it, even when your body is at rest. The mental image strengthens your knowledge, enabling you to hold the abstract thought. Enhancing comprehension through visualization might expedite the process. Dual coding may be necessary if a person can comprehend an idea better by following an image rather than just the words.

Simple visualization exercises can greatly increase enhancing your capacity for imagination will help you become more cre-

CHAPTER 11: VISUALIZATION AND CONCEPTUALIZATION

ative. To improve your abilities, use the following visualization approaches in the corresponding scenarios.

Visualization is a useful tool for solving all kinds of mathematical issues.

You might use imagery when attempting to comprehend the meaning of comprehension by adhering to the descriptive languages.

You can use visualization in accordance with the historical timeline to generate a detailed image of historical events by going over the list of historical events, together with their names and dates.

Visualization is a useful tool for comprehending abstract ideas.

To improve the level of visualization, you can adhere to the following crucial advice.

Poems should be read aloud and slowly. It will assist you in making a mental picture highly engaging language that is full of senses.

You should read aloud several times to make sure you understand the meaning of any unfamiliar words if you have trouble picturing the idea of a paragraph.

After reading one sentence, you should stop and use visualization to continue reading until you have understood each sentence individually. By closing your eyes or staring out the window, you can focus your mental image of the idea.

Every participant in a study group will provide their personal vision when explaining a certain idea. It contributes to a deeper comprehension of the idea.

No matter what you are reading or watching, you should constantly try to visualize the idea. Reading any kind of writing or viewing a movie, a documentary, or anything else.When attempting to comprehend a complex text's subject, recording your voice and reading slowly and loudly can be an effective strategy. Replaying the recording can help you get better at following along and using your imagination while you listen. You have the option to close your eyes while working on your visualization.

Methods for Simplifying Visualization

You have a basic, natural ability to visualize. Following through on the goal in order to succeed is something that most people do naturally throughout their lives. A person can achieve their dreams if they make a sincere effort to determine the practical route. You are able to perceive and feel what you produce in your visualize it in your head. By using the visualization technique, you can create mental images from whatever you read, hear, or sense. One of the most popular subconscious mental techniques, visualization, can help you get the true benefits of mindfulness practice. Visualization techniques can be used in a variety of contexts, including education, health, employment, sports, and more.

Using Visualization Techniques Frequently: The best method for developing visualizing skills is repetition. It is imperative that you envision frequently and remember to adhere to the predetermined plan. You can practice visualization on a regular basis at any time of day. Nonetheless, it's thought that the optimal times for meditating are right before and right after bed. You should continue to develop your mental picture consistently. It will assist you in more clearly and thoroughly visualizing.

Choose to Practice Visualization: No matter where you are, this is an option. You can begin working on your visualizing skills at any time or place. However, it's crucial that you make the decision to feel at ease while engaging in visualization exercises. Selecting your intended objective will allow you to begin constructing a natural image in a constrained space. After that, you ought to make an effort to broaden your thinking by sensing the environment. It will also assist you in lessening your nervousness before events.

Put yourself in the shoes of a targeted region: Visualization can be exercised by imagining yourself living in a specific area. It is a useful method for overcoming nervousness. and anxiety, which you may experience in relation to the particular issue. You ought to make an effort to move carefully through a humiliating phase. For instance, delivering a speech in front of an audience may make you anxious. It will make you feel more at ease and make it simpler for you to talk in public if you begin your speech by picturing yourself giving it in front of friends or other people you know. It is imperative that you educate yourself to deal with any scenario without fear.

Try Reading Mental Images Including Images: Using visualization techniques helps improve your comprehension and memorization abilities.

You can work on reading on your own or with a group to discover the variations and resemblances among the mental pictures that other people have created. Building a picture story from the material you have read is possible.

You can easily increase your knowledge by reading with visualization by adhering to these basic visualization techniques.

Applying Visualization for Reading Comprehension

If you are a beginner or find reading tough, you will need to acquire visualization strategies in order to become proficient in reading comprehension. People can visualize the stories they read by using visualization techniques. When reading comprehension, readers use their senses—including smell, sound, taste, sight, and touch—as well as their visualization skills to create mental images. When people are able to visualize the text, they focus on it. The reader can retain the text's contents in their memory thanks to visualization. A reader can use several visualization techniques to conjure up images in their head as they read about comprehension.

After listening, read: It is an excellent tactic to hear the text when The material is being loudly read by someone else. After then, you could try to visualize what you heard in the text. Following that, you can highlight or mark the passages in the text that helped you form the mental imagery. It is crucial to listen intently since it helps with learning a variety of skills, including integrating prior knowledge, picking up new languages, succeeding in school, and even finding success in the job. Reading and listening are closely related. You may raise your comprehension levels with listening exercises, and this will help you become a better reader.

A person's reading proficiency is influenced by two key aspects.

Vocabulary and background knowledge are these two crucial components. Should you possess a broad vocabulary, which will aid in both reading comprehension and text interpretation.

Choose an Audio Work to Work on Visualization: A person reading any literature may find it difficult to hear or recognize the words. Selecting an aural component is crucial; it might be a poem, children's rhyme, essay, or well-known song. Obtaining a great deal of information will aid with visualization.

Select a Crucial Aspect to Focus on: You can pick a certain text or story with vivid surroundings and evocative characters. It will make it easier for you to focus and use your visualization skills to understand the text's or story's meaning.

Choose a Nonfiction Narrative: You can increase your reading comprehension skills by using visualization. in line with nonfiction narratives. The factual story's incorporation of real-world aspects explains why. It is a simple concept for anyone to envision.

Easy Visualization Task

You can improve your creativity and broaden your imagination with these easy visualization exercises. To grasp any form of concept fast and effortlessly, you must have a high level of effective visualization.

Exercise with an Object: You must pay close attention to a thing. Closing your eyes will facilitate your thought process regarding the object. After then, you will rotate the object in your mind's eye and envision it thoroughly while taking into account various perspectives. You ought to take note of the object's surrounds as well.

Exercise with an image: You must study an image closely, and then close your eyes to create an image in your thoughts. You'll need to make an effort to remember the picture's background, surroundings, colors, and other details.

You'll need to take another look at the image so you can compare it to your mental image.

Exercise on Place: Consider the surroundings in which you live.

After that, you will fully focus on the setting you have chosen. To add more creativity to your visualization, use all of your senses to focus your attention on the object, as well as any sounds or odors related to the particular image.

Person Exercise: You must choose a person you are familiar with.

The next step will be to attempt to visualize that person. eyes, taking into account various circumstances and settings. You'll incorporate that person's range of facial emotions into the image. To exercise various people, repeat these processes.

CHAPTER 11: VISUALIZATION AND CONCEPTUALIZATION

Regulate Your Eye Movement

ADD/ADHD is typically diagnosed by physicians and parents when a patient experiences difficulty paying attention or learning new information. It may occur as a result of incorrect eye movement. When your eyes don't move smoothly, precisely, and accurately, you can have trouble with reading, writing, sports, and other activities. Furthermore, when trying to visualize anything, someone with weak eye movement will find it extremely difficult. Usually, the causes are issues with your eyes' accommodation, divergence, and convergence. of experiencing trouble moving the eyes.

Two primary categories of eye movements are associated with visualization.

Saccades: When you are observing different items, these eye movements, which resemble jerks, can assist you shift your visual attention. It clarifies your ability to see.

Pursuits: Using your vision skills, you must follow the object's movement when tracking anything.

Your eye movement problems can be resolved with certain treatments, which are administered.

Lenses: Using therapeutic lenses can occasionally help someone's eye movements. Lenses aid in sharpening focus when observing background or periphery things.

The main treatment for problems related to eye movements is vision therapy. **Syntonics:** This technique modifies an individual's eye movements by using various colored lights.

Give up subvocalizing

Sub-vocalization is a negative reading habit that forces the reader to concentrate on one word at a time instead of the concepts being given in full within several words. In general, subvocalization is unavoidable. There are a few efficient techniques you can use to break the subvocalization habit.

Here are some pointers to help you quit subvocalizing.

One can engage in repetitive practice by counting or by repeatedly saying a sentence. You'll read more quickly as a result.

When you are reading regularly, you have control over your eyes. However, you can jerk to move your eyes while reading if you feel like it. and it will influence how quickly you read. You can move your finger underneath each line in the context and sweep it from left to right. It will assist you in becoming more fluent readers, and eventually you will be able to read without using your finger.

Before reading the content carefully, you can briefly scan it. It will assist you in learning the unfamiliar words. You won't be as perplexed about what those terms signify once you start reading closely.

You can reduce the amount of subvocalization by using other sense organs like your lips, tongue, larynx, and ears as distractions. To distract your ears, turn on some calming tunes or rhythmic music on low level. You are able to Pick some chewing gum to take your mind off things.

There are primarily two types of sub-vocalization: high-vocalizers and low-vocalizers. You must lessen subvocalization if you wish to be an adept reader. Subvocalization hinders your ability to learn. Minimize subvocalization if you want to get better at reading. You experience lip movement and the usage of your natural voice during vocalization. On the other hand, when sub-vocalization occurs, you experience an inner voice while you work through a subject.

Subvocalization is typically a characteristic shared by readers who struggle to read anything. It also has an impact on understanding what you read and interpreting what you read.

12

CHAPTER 12: COMPREHENSION

There are various approaches you can use in order to understand any topic. The reader will need to draw connections between the information from other books and things that already exist in the real world and their prior knowledge. To grasp the true meaning of the text, the novel methods of thinking, or the novel creative styles, the reader will need to integrate new concepts or information with prior knowledge. The text will raise questions for the reader in their minds. The questions will center around how the reader responds to the book after reading it and why the author wrote it.

CHAPTER 12: COMPREHENSION

Reading is Comprehension

Understanding the content you are reading is represented by the act of reading comprehension. When you are reading, reading comprehension is crucial to the act of reading. Before beginning to read any text, during the reading process, and after finishing the reading, it demands your intention, activity, and information processing. The reader uses awareness of phonics and phonemes at the same time as having the capacity to decipher or organize meaning from the material they have read. The final step in the reading process is comprehension.

The progression of reading comprehension is influenced by two key components. The two main elements of reading comprehension are vocabulary knowledge and text comprehension. Your comprehension of the terminology utilized in the text is a crucial component. Should your lexicon be insufficient, you will need to continuously acquire new terms. It's also critical to comprehend each word's specific meaning inside the text so that you can combine word meanings to construct a coherent thought that has been explained within the text.

One of the main objectives of both reading and listening is comprehension. It aids in the information and skill acquisition of readers and listeners. Reading can be divided into four categories: intensive, scanning, extensive, and skimming. The phrase "skimming" refers to the simplest reading technique. In general, it's similar to having a cursory look at the issue. One kind is scanning. of reading that is a little more thorough and is typically applied when readers are attempting to locate a specific topic within the text.

The concept of comprehension is more scattered within the category of intensive reading. The reader will have to read every word in the text if they fall under the intensive reading category. Any unfamiliar word will need him or her to look up its definition. Being able to relate to the text is crucial for fully comprehending its meaning. When the reader is required to explain the ideas in the text in writing or voice, it is a useful method of reading. When readers want to read a material for enjoyment, they can adhere to the category of reading a lot. Your ability to comprehend comprehension will increase if you practice reading comprehension on a regular basis. For instance, reading comprehension practice will support a student's development of a fruitful academic career. There are a few potential causes for reading comprehension issues, including a lack of vocabulary, concepts, and other subtleties. If your vocabulary is small, your ability to use your imagination and your thoughts will be constrained.

There are numerous approaches to enhancing comprehension abilities in reading. These methods include summarizing, question-answering, story structure, collaborative learning, and comprehension monitoring.

Two strategies are involved in comprehension monitoring, which is a metacognitive process that involves comprehension of the text: regulation and evaluation. When someone reads aloud in a group or with another individual, It stands for group education. Occasionally, after reading the material, someone examines the possible inquiry pattern. Additionally, he or she will be able to compose the replies and they will symbolize responding questions.

Occasionally, after reading the material, a person gets better at reading comprehension and asks questions. In addition, after reading a text, readers construct stories with characters, actions, settings, problems, and objectives.

It aids in the development of their reading abilities. After reading the content, the readers can then summarize. When summarizing, he or she will need to perform a variety of duties, such as consider the key idea from the text, extrapolate from common examples, and focus on concepts that are repeated while excluding unimportant details.

Success is unattainable for an individual in their professional life as a result of their poor comprehension skills. When they read anything, these individuals are unable to absorb information. They have trouble understanding what they read, and they are unable to interpret the text.

Reading quickly requires focus

No matter what your line of work, it is imperative that you sharpen your reading comprehension. Speed reading is crucial if producing reports, proposals, periodicals, and letters is part of your professional work need. It will enable time savings for you. Additionally, it will help you improve your ability to focus. Here are a few strategies for reading quickly to sharpen your focus.

Avoid Being Sidetracked: Distractions should be avoided if you want to focus on the text you're reading. You have the option to turn off your TV, radio, and phone. To improve your concentration when reading, pick a calm area.

Learn to Prevent Rereading: You can educate yourself to prevent reading the same material more than once. You should practice reading each sentence aloud exactly once. After reading the completed lines, you can use an index card to cover them and drag it down the page. By using this strategy, you will be able to read more quickly and fully.

Regulate the Speed at Which You Read: Depending on the kinds of content you are reading, your reading pace may change. A newspaper or a magazine can be used as your reading material. Only the most significant headlines or information are visible to you. scanning of the single Reading key passages quickly might increase your reading speed.

You will need to pay closer attention when reading scientific or math books. You must read carefully as well. It will assist you in comprehending the material covered in these subjects, which also call for intelligence.

You ought to assess the subjects' priorities. By altering your reading habits, it will assist you in increasing your reading speed.

CHAPTER 12: COMPREHENSION

Reading quickly has many advantages, some of which are listed here.

Continue Reading Amount in Less Time: You can read more material in a shorter amount of time if you read more quickly. Thus, rapid reading is recommended if you are pressed for time and need to finish a large amount. is what will enable you to overcome it.

Improved comprehension as a result of Reading with Greater Depth and Perfection: You may read more deeply and perfectly when you read with complete focus. It will make it easier for you to comprehend the text's meaning.

High Level of Concentration: Reading any text more quickly will require a higher level of concentration. It will enable you to quickly concentrate on your idea.

Create an Information Collection for Better Reading: This will enable you to retain information in your mind more effectively when you are reading any material with intense focus. Appreciate Reading a Variety of Texts: You're going to be able to relish reading several different types of texts quickly. If you enjoy reading any kind of material, this will feed your mind.

Rapid reading of the text has further advantages. Here are these additional advantages.

Your habits of speed reading will enable you to browse the internet more effectively.

You may make your shopping more efficient by reviewing the nutrition facts on every product's label.

Reading the instructions quickly will help you operate or assemble an item.

As soon as you read the crucial components and planning information, you can quickly and sensibly create your strategy.

Your career can benefit from your speed reading skills. It will enable you to do your desk work in an office effectively. If you do your work on schedule, you'll get awards and possibly even a promotion.

If you work for a firm, you are required to keep a lot of business documents. To manage your firm effectively, you will also need to create reports and comprehend the content of various business documents quickly and readily.

CHAPTER 12: COMPREHENSION

Maximize Comprehension

Acquiring the skill of accurately reading and understanding written material is crucial. Maximizing your comprehension abilities will make your work more enjoyable and productive. You'll need to be proficient in both interpretation and

read through the materials' various topics. You can optimize your comprehension abilities when reading a material by putting the strategies listed below into practice.

Select the Most Effective Time of Day: You will need to consider when you are most comfortable putting your all into any task. It could be night, middle of the day, or dawn. You can maximize your comprehension skills by selecting this particular and effective time to read the literature of your choice.

Pick the Area That Will Produce the Most: You ought to locate find the perfect spot for you to complete your reading assignments. It might be your room, your office, a library, a café, and so forth. It is best to select a location where you can read with ease and comfort.

Avoid Distractions: Before beginning to read, switch off your email, Twitter, Facebook, and other digital distractions. You should also do this for a brief period of time while reading. You can let those who follow you know if you will be unavailable for a certain amount of time by stating so. It would be best if you made note of the time to prevent any interruptions from those individuals. As you read the text, you can listen to music. If you don't like listening to music when When reading, you can increase your concentration by using headphones without any music. It will support your effort to stay focused. People won't bother you because they'll assume you're engrossed in your reading.

Establish a Reading Prioritization Plan: The most significant portion of your reading should be your top priority, and you should begin reading from there.

You should read the text's easiest material after reading the most crucial portion. Create a reading strategy that makes the most of your understanding abilities.

Develop Your Vocabulary Knowledge: Understanding any material you read will be aided by the way words interact, form new words, and have context. If you know what each section of the sentence means, you will understand the overall meaning of the text. To get the most out of your reading comprehension, you will need to increase your vocabulary. You should choose a few unfamiliar terms from the text and research their definition and meaning. It will assist you in expanding your vocabulary.

Take Pleasure in Reading: One of the finest strategies to optimize comprehension abilities is to practice reading. It will be easier for you to love reading if you practice reading with enjoyment and enthusiasm. It will sustain your motivation. Additionally, it will give you more energy to read the content.

Your degree of engagement with the content will increase to the point where it maximizes your comprehension. You have an option. the book, which is suggested for readers a little younger than you. This kind of material will help you stay at ease, comprehend things more clearly, and develop better reading habits.

The aforementioned techniques for improving your comprehension skills should be followed if you wish to feel content, at ease, and like reading. Whether or not the reading is appropriate for your age level, you ought to participate in it. You could occasionally have trouble understanding certain passages or words. No matter how busy you are during the day, if you enjoy reading, you will find time to do it. In time, it will assist you in reaching your full comprehension potential. Additionally, it is It's critical to determine your areas of strength and weakness. By making improvements in the area where you struggle, you can increase your comprehension.

How to Improve Your Understanding Capabilities

It takes reading or hearing to fully experience and visualize the wide range of things that exist in this universe. Understanding what you read or listen to depends in large part on your comprehension abilities. There are a plethora of techniques for developing high comprehension abilities. These techniques can help you improve your understanding abilities.

Time and again Go over the text: Reading the book aloud will assist you in understanding new words and helping you decipher its meaning.

Make use of a dictionary in order to learn the definitions of new terms and record them in writing. You will be able to increase your comprehension by using this strategy.

Practice for Visualization: You should get comfortable fully seeing the text's contents as you read it. Once you have a mental picture of the subject matter of the text, you should also visualize it. It is a useful method for improving your understanding abilities. If creating a project presents difficulties for you, you should look for a method or fix that will assist you. To become more productive, you have to let fresh thoughts come into your head. For instance, you can recline in an armchair, close your eyes, and keep your hands on your lap. eyes or look out the window to take in the scenery outside. Additionally, you should keep an open mind and refrain from focusing on any one subject in particular. It will assist your mind in coming up with fresh writing concepts.

Establish a Connection with the Text: Make a comparison and determine how the text's subject relates to a number of aspects of your life. If there are any similarities to the text, it must enable you to make a connection with it. By developing your abilities, it will assist you in comprehending the text's meaning.

Develop a Question-Asking Habit: You ought to read the material carefully and develop the practice of asking more questions. You will need to use your analytical abilities to think carefully in order to come up with the solutions to these questions. Your understanding of the situation will improve as you analyze more, and your comprehension abilities will rise significantly.

Consider the Upcoming Events: It will be easier for you to comprehend the text's meaning if you always read it with full focus. You should attentively read the text's contents and try to plan out what will happen next. You can infer the events that will follow from the book if you read it attentively and passionately. As you get more proficient at doing that, reading challenging books will also appear more straightforward.

Maintain the Track by Accurately Interpreting the Meaning: You should proceed with reading the text by accurately comprehending its meaning and staying on course. You should pause reading if a particular passage in the text seems difficult for you to understand in order to get clarification. To grasp the meaning of those paragraphs, you can either read that particular section of the text more slowly or go over it again.

Summarize: After carefully reading the material, you should summarize it by noting its key points and then applying your own language to make the information in the text more broadly. Creating a synopsis of the material also relies on your vocabulary. In the event that you With a solid word bank, you'll be able to provide a precise and excellent synopsis of the work.

The more often you practice text summarizing, the better your skills will get.

Monitoring of Understanding Capabilities: distinct people have distinct reading preferences and modes of comprehension. When you read any text, you should pay attention to both your reading style and your comprehension skills. It will assist you in evaluating your procedures and making the necessary adjustments. Also, when reading any material, you ought to make an effort to identify the areas in which you struggle with comprehension.

CHAPTER 12: COMPREHENSION

Using Visual Aids to Improve Reading Comprehension

For reading comprehension, visualization is the process by which you create mental images in your thinking about the people and things that are in the book. The readers use their visualization skills when they employ their information and experiences to generate images. As they read, they fully imagine each character and experience the author's ideas about the material. They can also picture the text's color, feel its texture, smell it, and taste it as the author has described it.

When someone has trouble reading a text, they can see the alphabets on the page, but they are unable to connect the dots or decipher the text's hidden meaning. They are unable to visualize the content of what they read as a result. The visualization approach is dependent upon the capacity of the reader's mind to consider or visualize the subject that has been explained through the use of words in the text. Readers use the visualization technique to decipher textual meaning when they read a storybook. Following that, they develop or conceive the story's characters, as well as their surroundings and activities. Summarizing the material requires visualization as well. While reading, you might stop and consider the meaning in your own mind. After reading the material, you can talk about your thoughts and feelings with your companions.

When reading something without an accompanying visual, the reader will utilize their imagination to conjure up that particular image.

Should you cease his or her reading and ask them to clarify the information, you can determine how proficient they are in visualizing the scene. People who struggle with imagery will find it difficult to communicate what they have read. You will be able to appreciate the topic and comprehend its idea if you can adequately imagine it. Visualization is crucial if you want to apply what you've read to any subject.

If you have good visualization skills, you may eliminate distractions from your environment and discover all the relevant facts. A good visual aid also aids in accurate analysis of any subject. Proper visualization will provide you with multiple advantages for your career in the workplace as well. Numerous professional domains, including marketing, services, government finance, sports, education, and so forth, offer advantages.

How to Apply Maps

Mapping makes it easier to see what you are reading in the text and to make connections between the various personalities and details that are discussed.

Maintaining the subject in the center of the map canvas while organizing ideas, notes, and keywords around it is part of the mapping method. By employing mapping, you can enhance your cognitive abilities. You can use mapping to acquire visual learning strategies for identifying connections between the text's activities and elements. Additionally, it inspires a person to develop the concepts in the text by utilizing their own words. The procedures listed below must be followed while using mapping to aid with comprehension.

Gather General Data: Gathering information about the author, like name, address, background, and sources of inspiration for the book, is necessary before you begin writing comprehension. All of the details will enable you to make the connection between the text's explanation of the subject and the author's life. It will assist you in comprehending the main idea of the situation. Your comprehension of the subject is crucial to helping you envision it.

Consider the Characters: You'll have to make an effort to learn how the author developed the characters in relation to the plot. You can better understand the relationships between the various letters in the text by using a mapping technique.

Consider the Storyline: Using the plot's framework, you may determine the plot's location, which is indicated on the map.

Knowledge of Vocabulary: Reading comprehension depends on your vocabulary knowledge. You will need to include unfamiliar words as a separate vocabulary branch in your mind map.

Understanding of symbols and themes: You will need to include themes and symbols if you want an in-depth examination of the text. Every term in your mapping system needs to have its definition updated.

These are some of the places where mapping can be used. Taking notes is aided by mapping. You are forced to consider the crucial information that is provided when you use mind mapping. You can jot down significant details without going into great depth.

It is beneficial for text revision as well as helping you save time when reading.

Mind mapping is a useful tool for creating to-do lists. It will assist you in keeping in mind all the crucial details.

Reports and information presentations are both possible. It

also comes in handy when you have a speech to deliver because it keeps key information fresh in your memory. It can also be utilized to create a slide show.

There are instances when individuals are bored and lack enthusiasm for working on collective initiatives. Conscience mapping will enable them to participate fully and enthusiastically in group initiatives.

Visualization becomes easier with mapping. Learning the components and details needed to accomplish the goal as a group is beneficial. Assigning tasks to team members also helps.

Examining class notes is aided by mapping. It's a fantastic way to commit your lecture notes to memory. You may assemble mental links and add photos.

Planning ahead using a map facilitates exam preparation. It is beneficial to have all of the materials you will need for your test in one place.

A reading list consisting of lecture notes, book chapters, and other materials can be included. To maintain notes and organize your thoughts about the exam and other tasks, you can utilize a mind map.

Mapping helps by offering ideas to compose an essay. It enables you to get data for writing essays from various sources.

Furthermore, it will help you organize the essay's outline. Both creativity and productivity are increased by mind mapping. It facilitates the generation of fresh concepts and improves comprehension of connections among the information and data that are at your disposal. It's a great technique to maintain the originality and precision of your thoughts. It saves time and enables you to obtain ideas rapidly.

One of the greatest ways to arrange your ideas and classify them based on their unique characteristics is to use mapping.

Additionally, you can fit a lot of concepts onto a single page, giving you the ability to quickly review a lot of material. You can use keywords, colors, and images to make a mental map. It encourages you to remember crucial information and aids in improving your memory. By enabling the full comprehension of your brain, mapping provides an explanation for your brilliant thinking.

CHAPTER 13: SPEED WRITING SKILLS

It's likely that you will come across individuals in your life that can be considered writing machines, but do you want to emulate them as well? It's not too difficult because practice is all you need. However, wringing quicker just for the purpose of doing so will not help you much. You have to write more quickly without sacrificing any of the content's quality. Nobody would want to read what you've written, for instance, if it is poorly readable and full of grammatical errors. Consequently, this chapter will teach you the things to remember while also improving your writing pace.

CHAPTER 13: SPEED WRITING SKILLS

Grammar

In this realm of online self-expression, the internet has completely transformed the means and limitations of human communication. You can write informally on the internet, but formal English—of which grammar is a crucial component—is what you'll need to know for everything else in life.

Sentence Construction

Some people believe that there should be no restrictions on their writing, but in the end, guidelines are supposed to give your work a certain quality that you can appreciate. The framework is the most crucial component of any writing, whether it be brilliant prose or an educational blog. And to do that, you must be knowledgeable about appropriate sentence structure techniques. Consider a puzzle with all the parts put in the incorrect order. Do you find it to be nice? Not at all, correct? The reason for this is because while the dispersed pieces won't come together to make a picture, they will appear harmonic and ideal when arranged properly. This also holds true for a sentence. The sentence won't make sense if the words are not placed correctly. Thus, even when you are writing quickly, you must remember that sentence structure cannot be sacrificed.

Tense

Tension is something that communicates the details of what happened when, as you undoubtedly already know. It's crucial to understand dominant tenses in order to properly construct your sentences. Tenses can be broadly classified into three categories: past, present, and future tenses. These can now be divided into even more categories. However, the majority of writing mistakes have to do with these tenses.

You also need to understand the various grammatical viewpoints. For instance, different tenses will be used depending on whether the activity is ended or still in progress.**Singular or Plural Words**

Nowadays, everyone assumes that I'm talking about one or many when I use the terms single or plural. But these words have other uses as well. In the instance of subject-verb agreement, they are also employed. In this instance, the verb you used in the sentence will be chosen depending on how many nouns it contains. You must first determine if the noun is solitary or plural in order to compose the phrase correctly. You should be aware of several unusual situations where even plural nouns are handled as though they were singular. Take news, for instance. An additional item that It's important to remember that most collective nouns are singular even though they may sound multiple. This is so because they are employed to denote a group of objects when the group is unique in and of itself. Take the crowd, for instance.

Next are non-countable words, such as "water." Since it is impossible to count, it is always regarded as singular.

Indefinite and Definite Articles

Every sentence has an article, and they play a crucial role in it. Even though they are tiny, they have a big impact. They are always in front of a noun. Usually, the article is used to indicate whether a noun is singular or plural, generic or specialized. Articles come in two varieties: definite and indefinite. Again, there are two forms for indefinite articles: singular (a, an) and plural (some). You should use an indefinite article if you are making a first-time or general reference to something in your writing. However, keep in mind that "a" is used for consonants and "an" for vowels. The definite article "the" is the sole one in English grammar that is used in cases of terms in the single and plural. It can also be applied to nouns that have already been introduced in written form. Even when writing quickly, selecting the appropriate article is crucial to getting the point across.

Contractions

Words that have one or more letters removed to make them shorter are known as contractions. An apostrophe is used when writing these words to make up for the letters that are dropped. For instance, they'll, can't, won't, and so on. Now, contractions are not always used in writing; that is, they are not utilized in official writing, but they are frequently used in informal writing, particularly in situations where space is at a premium, such as in advertisement copies.

In everyday talks, contractions are frequently used, therefore you may find yourself inclined to employ them in your speed writing to save time. However, keep in mind the style of writing that you are carrying out. Under formal circumstances, contractions should be avoided. Additionally, contractions can be used to retain a colloquial tone in informal writing.

Conjunctive

The word "conjunctive" is used to refer to linking verbs, sometimes known as "be" verbs in everyday speech. Conjunctive adverbs, on the other hand, are employed to link concepts and include words like "consequently" and "however." It is crucial to use punctuation correctly while using conjunctions.

Spelling

Spelling errors are among the most frequent errors made by anyone when writing quickly. You are not alone in making these errors; even native speakers do! You will require your spelling abilities throughout your life. Even when you write quickly, your writing will be useless if all of your spelling errors are in. Thus, you should bear the following points in mind if you want to spell correctly.**Know the rules**

The English language has a set of standard spelling conventions that apply to it. You won't benefit from attempting to memorize them all at once, and you won't be able to recall all of them correctly, so try not to put too much pressure on yourself. Therefore, the easiest method to learn about these rules is to take some time each day to review a few words and determine whether they adhere to any specific rules. For instance, when you type "friendliness," the "y" that appears in the word "friendly" will become a "i." This rule states that if a word's final letter is "y," adding a suffix to it will cause it to shift to a "i," however suffixes that begin with "i," like "-ing," are exempt from the requirement. Since "-ness" is the suffix in this case, the rule is applicable.

Make a list of words that you find difficult to spell

Everybody has encountered terms in their lives that they find challenging to spell. Not everyone will necessarily need to hear these words the same way. However, you've should give it careful thought and compile a list of the terms you frequently misspell or neglect to spell correctly. Additionally, these may be uncommon words, so you may not always be certain of how they are spelled. It's okay if they appear easy. There is no rivalry here. Since you developed the list for your own use, you are free to include anything on it. This is a crucial phase since it requires you to determine what it is that you actually need to learn.

Prepare a list of words that are commonly misspelled

Create a different list, separate from your own, with words that are frequently misspelled. You can obtain these lists by searching the internet or YouTube. There may be lengthy lists that you encounter; however, you are not obliged to become familiar with them all. To ensure that you do not make any mistakes when writing quickly, I would like you to list all of these terms in your notebook or journal and then periodically review them.

Reading books will always help

I'm sure you're wondering how reading relates to our discussion on speed writing. That's all there is to it. Reading aids in helping you commit a word's appearance on paper to memory. Additionally, as you read more, you will encounter these words more frequently and eventually learn the correct form of each word, so you won't make any mistakes. You'll eventually learn that spelling is more about a word's appearance than its pronunciation. You will therefore gain a great deal from reading a variety of novels.

Look out for word origins

Words used in writing are not exclusively English. A few of them also have Greek or Roman ancestry. Looking up a term's origin in a dictionary will not only improve your comprehension of the word but also aid in spelling memory.

Break down the words

Words that are overly long are frequently the ones that are misspelled the most. The best method to learn them if you have the same issue is to break knocking them down. For the obvious reason that you are chunking the term rather than using it in its entirety, the technique is also known as chunking. For instance, "astonishing" can be rewritten as "as-ton-ishing" by breaking it down. You can do this with almost any word that you find challenging to spell.

Play word games

Finally, word games are a great way to learn and retain spellings as well as expand your vocabulary. You may purchase a plethora of vintage board games for this use, with Scramble being the most popular. Additionally, there are a number of spell-testing apps like SpellTower that you might utilize if you have an interest in technology.

It is now your responsibility to get going and use these suggestions; you should experience the benefits in a few days.

Punctuation

A written work is never complete without the appropriate punctuation, and if you use it incorrectly, occasionally the meaning can even be entirely changed. Visualize the circumstances around your speech. Do you use the same tone of voice the entire time? No, since you have to either strike a stance or alter your tone of voice to make a sentence make sense. Similarly, even while writing quickly, you still need to employ punctuation if you want the readers to grasp the precise sense of what you

CHAPTER 13: SPEED WRITING SKILLS

are saying. For instance, when you say, "Time to eat, kids!" you are informing your children that mealtime is approaching. However, if the punctuation is removed, the statement looks like this.

It's time to eat, young people! and this implies that you wish to consume the children! So you can see how much of an influence even a single comma can have. In essence, punctuation is the usage of a wide variety of marks and symbols. You were only able to discern the significance of the comma in the case above. There are additional uses for commas. A comma is used, for instance, if you want the reader to see that there is a pause. In list-making, commas are essential even in this situation. The full stop, which is equally crucial, follows.

It's likely obvious to you, but to be explicit, it denotes that a phrase is coming to a conclusion can proceed to your following sentence. In some contexts, abbreviations are also indicated with a single full stop. For instance, the letters Nov. and Tel. No. stand for November and telephone number, respectively.

The exclamation point is another symbol that you can use to convey strong emotions in a text. Anything can trigger it, including love, fear, sorrow, or rage. Additionally, it can be used to indicate a direct or urgent instruction. For instance, "Stop!" Another thing to keep in mind while employing exclamation points is that a full stop is not necessary if you are utilizing them. When writing informally, using an exclamation point to highlight a sentiment is acceptable, however Even so, use cautious when using it. Additionally, the symbol should be avoided as much as possible in professional or semi-formal language.

Let's now discuss the question mark. Probably the easiest one is this one.

It is always used at the conclusion of a statement and is employed when posing some queries. There's no need for a full stop here either. "What did you have for breakfast?" for instance

The semi-colon and colon come next, and it's common for individuals to mix them up. I suppose the semicolon is the hardest punctuation mark to use and put appropriately out of all of the others. When you combine two phrases that have a relationship to if they relate to one another in any manner, a semicolon can be used. For instance, "We decided to have the picnic today since it looks like a nice day." However, if you are unsure about the appropriate placement of the semicolon, do not use one at all and divide the sentence in half instead. Conversely, the colon is employed to provide a clear stop in your writing, usually between two phrases. When you are about to begin a list, that is when you employ a colon the most. For instance, "The reasons for this decision are as follows:"; nevertheless, it is also evident in the case of a title that is descriptive, such as the one for this book.

CHAPTER 13: SPEED WRITING SKILLS

Tips to Double Your Writing Productivity

After learning the fundamentals that you must remember when you practice speed writing, you also need to be aware of various writing tricks that can help you write more effectively. Go on to learn more.**Fix a particular technique of writing**

Your handwriting has a significant impact on how quickly you write. Your writing speed will increase if you focus on making your handwriting better. Your forearm and shoulder muscles should be used to manipulate your pen; your fingers should only serve as a guide. This method guarantees that you won't wear out quickly. You will write more slowly if you stop wriggling your wrist so much.

Try to maintain a proper posture

Maintaining good posture is another way to increase writing speed. It need to be something you're at ease with. Your back should be supported by a chair, and your feet should be flat on the floor. This is the perfect stance. Refusing to give in to the habit of slouching can eventually generate tension on your arm, which will reduce your pace. The height of your workstation and chair are also crucial considerations.

When your desk and chair are too high for you, it can be especially harder to write more quickly or with good posture.

Don't grip the pen too hard

People often grip their pen too tightly when they're trying to write rapidly. However, you'll slow down and tire out your hands from this. Therefore, you should monitor your pen grip and make sure it is not too tight even while you are writing. However, if you continue to hold it excessively tightly even after several tries, it's time to acquire a decent one that will provide you a solid grip.

Hold your pen in a way that is comfortable to you

Finally, how you hold your pen will have a big influence, so find a position that is comfortable for you. Also, the grip on your pen becomes especially crucial if you are someone who must write for prolonged periods of time.

Having legible handwriting increases automaticity when writing. Additionally, you might choose to study shorthand according on the type of work you are performing, as it is a very helpful skill for office work.

Different Styles of Writing

Not only is there one kind of writing, but there are several types of writing, including speed writing. If you want to do it correctly, you must be aware of all these varieties before you start your speed writing journey.

Formal and Informal Writing Styles

The main distinction between these two writing styles is the readership you are writing for. You can employ an informal writing style if you can feel at ease with your audience and they are someone you know well. There are a lot more contractions and abbreviations used in these types of writing. Conversely, formal writing requires the use of longer words, a well-organized appearance, and the avoidance of slang. Exclamations are definitely prohibited in formal writing, as was previously mentioned.

When to Use Formal and Informal Writing?

You may be wondering when to apply these now that you

have a basic understanding of them. However, you must first dispel a common misconception: formal writing is superior to informal writing in many respects. This is not a competition, so it is completely incorrect. Each has its own use, as well as distinct styles. Formal writing is chosen when writing for a professional audience; nevertheless, casual writing is utilized while communicating with acquaintances. You may observe that certain individuals are less formal in their emails, but that is untrue. Avoid engaging in "informals" even while sending your client an email.

Informal Writing Styles

- **Colloquial** – As you undoubtedly well know, the term "colloquial" here refers to a casual way of speaking in the community. You may refer to it as conversational writing in certain instances, but in others, you just have to follow the rules. When you are confronting someone on the issue of water, you can even adopt a direct and intimate tone.
- **Simple** – One such kind of casual writing is thought to be simple writing. The majority of the sentences in this passage are brief and structured to convey a message. Sometimes, these little statements may even seem incomplete to you. To put it briefly, it's a highly informal style of writing. You will need to clarify and break down any industry jargon if you are required to mention it.
- **Contractions and Abbreviations** – Both contractions and abbreviations can be found in informal writing, as you have already learnt in the previous section of this chapter. Can't, she'll, he'll, they'll, and won't are a few of the contractions that are most frequently used in the English language. In an informal writing piece, you may encounter several

abbreviations. Common examples include Co. for company, Dr. for doctor, No. for number, and so on.
- **Empathy and Emotion** – These two characteristics are also frequently observed in casual writing. When you write with empathy, it indicates that you have placed yourself in the reader's position and are aware of their feelings. As a result, your work will naturally connect with readers.

One of the most important things to remember is who your audience is. Only one audience segment at a time can you relate to on an emotional level. Therefore, you cannot abruptly alter your audience midway through a book that you are writing. Therefore, the reason your book, blog, or anything else you've published hasn't gotten a lot of attention is because your readers didn't connect with you. It won't matter if you finished your piece ahead of time and submitted it for a competition if it lacks empathy, which gives the judges the impression that you have truly been able to leave your mark.**Formal Writing Styles**

- **Complex** – Generally, sentences written in the formal style are longer. All of the topics you choose to write about should be thoroughly researched, and this extends to everything you write. Each major topic in your writing must be expanded upon, and an introduction and conclusion must be included. Abstraction is not permitted. Everything needs to be concrete, logical, well-structured, and visually appealing. Additionally, you want to be aware of the distinction between lengthy sentences and ambiguous language. Long sentences are required, but that doesn't always mean your sentences have to be ambiguous. They ought to be intelligible to everyone.

- **Objective** – Each major point you plan to make in your formal writing should be clearly stated and backed up by ample evidence. Here, your feelings shouldn't take the stage. Actually, professional writing uses few or no expressive punctuations. You need to express your ideas clearly and succinctly. There shouldn't be any extraneous words or filler sentences included merely to boost the word count. There shouldn't be any generalizations. To ensure that the reader understands everything, everything should be made clear. All questions should be addressed in the content itself.
- **Full Words** – When writing in a formal style, contractions and abbreviations are not appropriate. If you must write "He will," do it in its whole rather than just "he'll." Additionally, you ought to spell out abbreviations if you are forced to use them and are unable to avoid them. This should only be done once. The next time, you can use the acronym, but attempt to use it less frequently. This rule only applies to a select few, and even then, only to those who are more widely recognized by their acronyms than by their entire names. NATO, for instance, the BBC, and so forth. Only use conversational English when using a lot of contractions and abbreviations.
- **Third Person** – In contrast to formal writing, which lacks any personal element, informal writing is more intimate. You should avoid hurting people's sentiments when writing in a formal style.

Regarding your personal self, you ought to express "disconnected from the writing." As a result, the third person becomes even more crucial. To add extra meaning, the word "you" has to be changed to one of several different proper nouns. When referring to third-person, terms like "everyone," "no one," and "someone" are also recommended. Gender stereotypes should be avoided at all costs. The assumption that doctors cannot be women might arise if you said, "The doctor gives his patients candy." It is thought to be a remarks that are sexist. There is no greater method for objectivity and adaptability than employing a third-person narrative. Your writing will cease to be personal with third-party usage, and formal writing styles require precisely that.

14

CHAPTER 14: WRITING FOR STUDY

When contrasting various writing styles, academic writing stands out as being very distinct from other types of writing you have done in the past. This chapter will cover the fundamentals and provide you with advice on how to improve your English language proficiency for academic purposes. By the time this chapter ends, you will understand how to structure and assess your own essays and dissertations.

Academic Writing

The final goal of a piece of writing greatly influences all forms of writing. When writing a research paper, for instance, your writing style is very different from that of narrating a narrative or sending a letter to a friend. Academic writing is commonly defined as the type of writing used in college and university assignments and research papers related to a specific subject. The fundamental tenet of academic writing is that all other content must revolve around a primary subject. Without any reiterations or side trips, your primary subject serves as the foundation for your argument. Any type of academic writing's primary goal is not to amuse readers, but rather.

Formality

The first guideline for writing in an academic setting is that the tone of the writing should be official. As a result, your writing shouldn't sound conversational or informal. A precise vocabulary is essential, and some terms—such as slang, idioms, colloquialisms, and even journalistic expressions—should be avoided at all costs. Since colloquial and informal language are inherently seen as inaccurate means of communication, there is typically a great deal of distortion attached to them. Furthermore, non-native English speakers frequently struggle to comprehend colloquial language. Since they are informal, terms like "stuff," "sort of," and so on should not be utilized.

For instance, writing "the business leaders of the country" is ideal for an academic essay; however, writing "the business heavyweights of the country" is too casual and unsuitable for academic writing.

Complexity

You'll also note that spoken language is generally much

simpler than written language. The primary cause of this is the abundance of lengthier words, richer meanings, and a diverse vocabulary. There is a greater emphasis on nouns than verbs in the sentences utilized. As a result, academic writing has far greater grammatical intricacy. Additionally, there are more subordinate clauses and passives. In summary, academic writing is far more sophisticated when seen through the lens of grammar. Additionally, there are more lexical varieties.

Precision

Because everything in an academic piece of writing is expected to be exact, figures and facts must be provided only after thorough verification. There must also be a lot of facts and numbers, and no ambiguous word combinations—such as "a source stated"—should be used. You must cite your source and state who stated what.

Objectivity

For good reason, objectivity is frequently regarded as the most difficult component of academic writing. When you write academically, you'll notice that your writing frequently focuses more on your beliefs and feelings than on the actual world.

Therefore, the primary reason for maintaining neutrality in your work is that the information that is offered ought to be the focal focus. The topic or impartiality of your written work shouldn't be based on your thoughts or opinions about the subject. Your instructor or professor is not interested in your opinions or thoughts when they assign you a task; rather, they are interested in the facts that you can find.

As a result, you should refrain from use expressions like "in my opinion" and instead focus more on the facts rather than attempting to evoke an emotional response from your audience. To put it succinctly, academic writing must have an impersonal tone. Thus, you will not be referring to the jobs or acts that you are mentioning as being performed by you. Additionally, "you" or the other person must be avoided. However, you will need to employ personal pronouns in your writing for some specific types of writing, such as reflective writing. Therefore, the greatest method to make sure you completed everything correctly is to consult.

However, I can offer you some advice if you're unsure about how to write without utilizing the first or second person. The passive voice is the first method that may be used. Using the third person is the second approach.

Finally, you may make objects the topic of your sentences rather than individuals.

Accuracy

One of the most important requirements for all forms of academic writing is accuracy in both terminology and statements made. Certain terms, such as "cash" and "money," might be used interchangeably when speaking in daily conversation since they are frequently confused. However, not all terms may be used in that way in an academic article. Each of these phrases has a distinct meaning and context, so you must use caution while use them. You could think they all signify the same thing at first appearance, but deeper examination reveals that they have different uses in addition to unique ones.

How to Write an Essay?

Writing an essay for the first time might be intimidating for a novice.

But understanding how to write an essay is crucial for a variety of reasons, whether you're a student or even working. It will be necessary for you to know for a number of formal presentations and even while applying to other institutions. The easiest method to get proficient with it is to divide it up into little jobs so that it doesn't appear as daunting. An essay is a brief piece of writing in which you must clearly state your position on the subject and provide as much information as possible. Continue reading to get a step-by-step tutorial on writing essays.

Step 1 – Pick a topic

Of course, choosing a topic to write about is the first step. However, you must first choose the kind of essay you wish to write. The many kinds are as follows:

- Essays that tell stories are quite simple and easy to write, so if you're just starting out, you should definitely give them a go. These articles' primary goal is to spread knowledge, but they do it in a methodical and narrative way.
- Essays that explain anything step-by-step are known as explanatory essays. To put it briefly, they are known as how-to essays.
- Essays that aim to persuade the reader are known as persuasive essays. They are written from a certain point of view.
- Essays that are descriptive tend to concentrate on the specifics. It might be about a special day in your life or your trip to the Maldives. Whatever the case, though, the

specifics must be stated.
- Argumentative essays are written on contentious subjects, and you must argue either in favor of or against the subject. It resembles a discussion in several ways, but it's written.

Step 2 – Brainstorm ideas

It's time to consider what precisely you want to write once you've decided on a topic and the style of essay you want to write. At this stage, all you do is ponder. You can start by taking a sheet of paper and listing anything that is on your mind, in brief. Your in-depth analysis of the subject will be aided by the entire procedure. To come up with ideas for your topic, you can browse the internet or books from libraries.

Step 3 – Create your outline

It's time for you to create an outline after you have outlined the things you wish to include. Alternatively, you may use the flowchart system for this.

In the middle of a page, write the topic. After that, you may create branches that will take you to the many topics you choose to cover. Additionally, you have the option to number them based on your desired order of mention or importance. Another method for making an outline that is more straightforward requires you to separate the essay into three sections: the introduction, the body, and the conclusion. You then need to arrange your ideas into each of these three columns. This will provide you with the framework for your essay.

Step 4 – Decide your thesis statement

It's time to begin writing the essay now that you have the topic and the basic structure, or outline, of it. The creation of a thesis statement is the initial stage in this multi-step procedure. This sentence essentially helps the readers understand why you are writing the essay. However, you should look over your outline again to make sure you have a clear understanding of your point of view and what you want to express in order to come up with a strong thesis statement.

The thesis statement should contain your essay's general reaction to the topic you wish to explore.

Step 5 – Compose the introduction

It's time to provide the introduction now. This ought to be attention-grabbing and compelling enough to keep readers' interest from the first line to the last. It's important to keep in mind that the beginning is the section of the essay where the reader must be won over, since a poor impression might occasionally result in the reader disliking the entire work. Put simply, the opening should always be the main emphasis of your essay rather than the body. Even if you could have written the finest body of writing, the introduction was uninteresting. Since the introduction is the initial impression, this won't draw in many readers.

Step 6 – Write the body

The body is where you have to go into further information about your topic. Examine the outline that you created before. Now, take up each of the ideas or branching topics you mentioned and expand on them in the body of the essay. Every paragraph in the body should have the same general format. Each justification you provide for your assertions and points of contention has to be solidly backed. When discussing many smaller concepts, they should all be connected as a single notion by utilizing a number of related bits of information.

Step 7 – Write the conclusion

This is the section where you must provide an overview of your ideas. Here, your main goal should be to provide a concluding analysis of what you have previously covered in the essay. It shouldn't be too long, but it has to have a few powerful lines that support your main idea. Read it again once you've written it down to make sure the closing was completed correctly and that there are no loose ends. The essay shouldn't come out as haphazard.

Step 8 – Do a grammar check

Even if you could believe that your work is over when you write the conclusion, your grammatical check is still ongoing. Errors and typos will only cause problems for the essay's correctness and clarity, not to mention negatively impact the reader's experience. Look for any spelling mistakes of any kind. The most frequent kind of ignored issue is when a word is misspelled correctly but the spelling checker does not catch it since it is still a word. For instance, "in" and "inn."

CHAPTER 14: WRITING FOR STUDY

How to Write a Report?

Occasionally, you will be required to create a report for your academic assignment rather than an essay. Additionally, in the event that you are a professional, your senior manager may request that you give a report on a certain facet of the business. So, if you're not sure which writing style to utilize, this is a quick summary of all you need to know.

Step 1 – The terms of reference should be decided first

Selecting the terms of reference for your report—that is, the topics it will be based on—is the first stage in the process. You must first remember any and all of the instructions or information that you have already been given. Determining the goal of your report will be the primary objective. Therefore, you should question yourself what your report will be about initially. The next thing you must determine is what you need and why you need the report in the first place. It is also necessary to determine who the report's intended audience is.

Step 2 – Figure out the procedure

This section focuses on the investigation and the steps you must take to prepare the report. Thus, you must first determine the kind of information you require. This may or may not entail a background investigation. Additionally, you must locate the papers or publications you need to go through in order to gather data for your report. Next, determine if the information you are receiving is adequate or if you require further help from the library. Next, ascertain if conducting an interview is necessary, and ultimately, decide on the best course of action.

Step 3 – Research

Now that you have decided on your strategy, it is time to carry out the real investigation. However, you need to confirm that there is no improper content or fraud when you do locate the information. You must be accurate with your facts and information. It is also necessary for you to periodically review the standards and criteria in order to stay on course. Should you be unfamiliar with the marking scheme (should the report be considered a university assignment), please get in touch with your instructor right once.

Step 4 – Frame the structure

A report needs to adhere to a specific format. There are several popular report categories, including business, lab, research, investigative, and so on. The sort of report you are writing will undoubtedly influence the format. The length and level of formality required for the report determine its structure next.

Reports follow the conventional structure of introduction, body, and conclusion. A report must also have the following other elements: findings, a title page, contents, an executive summary, a procedure, suggestions, references, and so forth.

Step 5 – Start drafting

It's time for you to begin the drafting process. The headers must be written down first. Please complete any other forms that need to be filled out.

Your report's foundation is its results. These comprise your research, conversations, findings, and any related materials. Tables, pictures, and graphs may even be included; however, this will rely on a number of factors, including the nature of your report. You may also begin building the appendix side by side. You must add in this section any material that is too lengthy to be contained in the main body. You may also include any other information that needs to be included with the report here.

Step 6 – Analyze your findings

The next thing you need to do is analyze or evaluate your most recent results.

After you have thoroughly reviewed the analysis, you may ask yourself a few questions to ensure that you have completed the analysis. The first query should go without saying: you should ask yourself precisely what you have discovered. Next, determine the relevance or importance of your results. Next, see what your research indicates. For instance, your research or observations may reveal the reason behind a certain incident.

Step 7 – Write the recommendations

Here's where you have to write what you believe ought to be done. As a result, you are either outlining the future course of action or providing a fix for the current issue. However, you should review your results again if you are unsure about what to write. Furthermore, your suggestions shouldn't be ambiguous or nonsensical. They ought to be useful. Your report should have all the information required for the explanations so that your reader is not left in the dark.

Step 8 – Write the executive summary and the contents

While it's not always necessary, the executive summary is occasionally needed. In addition, the table of contents has to be completed. Yes, these two pieces will be included at the beginning, but they must be completed last. The summary, which is often no more than 100 words, is essentially a condensed version of the information you hope to convey throughout your report.

Step 9 – Form the reference list

Every source you consulted for information must be included, and APA reference style is often used.

Step 10 – Revise

Finally, to ensure that there are no errors, you must rewrite the full report. Verify that all of the recommendations have been followed by reading them over again. After then, there ought to be no informational gaps. You also need to make sure that your argument makes sense. Additionally, you want to define each acronym and unique phrase you employ in the report. There needs to be clarity and a high level of readability. The labels on the diagrams need to be accurate. Every heading and numbering system has to be formatted correctly.

Journalistic Writing

Writing news stories is a type of journalistic writing if it interests you. Do you have trouble knowing where to begin? If so, you've come to the correct spot as everything you need to accomplish is broken out step-by-step here.

Step 1 – Find a subject to write about

Selecting an engaging topic to write about is among the first things you need to accomplish when writing for a journalistic audience. The degree to which readers adore the subject will determine how well-received your piece is.

Step 2 – Conduct interviews

The first step in writing as a journalist is to conduct interviews with pertinent persons.

You must first search the public for resources related to your topic of choice. But before you do, prepare who to contact and do some independent research. Only then will your interview go well. You ought to have a pen and paper on hand. Here's a little tip: since it appears to work better, always conduct the interview like a conversation. Three to five sources is the optimal amount for your article.

Step 3 – Practice good reporting

Regardless of your level of writing proficiency, you must practice sound reporting techniques. There's little doubt that some questions are on your readers' minds. Once you've determined what those questions are, you need to conduct the interview so that each one is adequately addressed. Additionally, since journalistic writing relies heavily on accuracy, you should double-check all of the material you have. Additionally, the name of the source must be correct and free of typos.

Step 4 – Make use of good quotes

Make a note of any inspirational statement you come across during your interviews. It's true that not all of the quotations will fit, and occasionally some may not even seem to apply. Therefore, it would be best if you put all you have learned in writing. There will be flat quotes and captivating quotes. You must use quotes with the ability to captivate the audience if you want to develop the tale.

Step 5 – Be fair and objective

In the event of news reports, opinion-spreading is not permitted. They must possess strength, bravery, and justice. Even if you may have strong feelings about the subject you have selected, this does not indicate that your writing will be prejudiced. You must put your emotions aside and report from the perspective of an impartial observer. It's important to focus on what your sources have said rather than what you believe.

Step 6 – Your lede should be great

Nobody will look at your tale again if the lede is not attention-grabbing or captivating. Your article's success will mostly depend on how wonderful and jaw-dropping your lede is. Your story's lede is what will set it apart from the competition and entice people to read it. Finding your story's point of interest and then communicating it to your audience are the first steps in crafting the ideal lede.

Step 7 – Structure your story

It's time to organize the remainder of the tale after you have resolved the lede. The ability to effectively and succinctly deliver the most information possible is what makes a news article great. There also has to be complete clarity. Most individuals adhere to a specific structure that specifies that your tale should be presented in the shape of an inverted pyramid.

This implies that the most information need to be presented at the beginning of the tale and the least amount at the conclusion.

Step 8 – Mention the sources properly

Nobody will trust your narrative if you don't cite the original sources from which you derived it. There will be trust in your article when you are transparent about your sources. Additionally, you'll be able to gain your readers' confidence. You can also attempt to include the on-record attribution, if that is feasible.

Step 9 – Check for any errors with your AP format

Even if you have produced a fantastic article, it will never be complete if it is not proofread for AP style problems. AP style is widely accepted as the standard for journalistic writing. If you are not familiar with it already, this is the first thing you should do. The AP style should be simple to learn. Your AP stylebook should be close at hand in case you need to refer to it. All of the common AP styles will come easily to you with practice and patience.

Step 10 – Keep a follow-up story ready

Once your article is complete and submitted to your editor, it's time to prepare a follow-up piece as well. It may initially appear difficult. All you have to do is consider the outcomes or causes that your tale has addressed. You will eventually generate enough material for your next narrative.

CHAPTER 15: SPEEDWRITING FOR FASTER NOTE-TAKING

You will need to be an excellent listener if you wish to learn rapid writing.

Brief notes are essential for writing quickly. Another crucial component of fast writing is having a strong memory. Gathering facts is a prerequisite before beginning any writing. Once you finish this chapter, you will have mastered the art of taking notes more quickly by using the many strategies listed here.

Note Taking from Reading

Since you read newspapers and magazines for enjoyment or relaxation, reading them is typically referred to as passive exercise. However, reading for study purposes is referred to be an active exercise as the goal is to enhance your understanding via reading. Making notes is a useful strategy for engaging with your reading actively. You will need to consider the ideas presented in the text when taking notes after reading it. You also attempt to determine how best to articulate them.

The first thing to do when considering taking notes is to consider why you are taking them. It is usually helpful to have a solid note in order to comprehend the challenging passages in the text. Making good notes when reading the literature aids in structuring the data and concepts you take away from it. Remaining engaged and maintaining concentration while reading is beneficial. By keeping a record of the things you have read, you may make it easier for yourself to find these things later on. Making a note also facilitates understanding the text's major themes and conclusion. Having a solid basis before delivering a speech is also beneficial.

You can follow the steps given below to take note after reading.

- You should make a list of bullet points summarizing the chapters you have read after you have finished reading them. If there are any questions in the text that need to be addressed, you should highlight that paragraph. You will then set it aside for a week.
- Read over all of the notes in your book one more. You'll record the page number of any important notes and store them within your book. There are occasions when you can

mentally summarize a key point made in the text.
- You can review the content and the notes you've previously gathered after a few days. After reading the material, you should attempt to draw connections and examine the topics you have learned.

You should read the material with whole concentration while using it as a source for notes. It will make it simple for you to identify the main ideas. The keywords you choose or emphasize for your note-taking require extra caution. As soon as you finish reading the text, you should try to identify the important terms. To rapidly make notes, you can either highlight or underline the relevant textual content. People will occasionally write quick remarks in the magazine or text's margin. It is undoubtedly a bad idea because the content or magazine could not belong to you. Notes can be used as a photocopy.

You may create your vocabulary on a note-taking sheet separately. You are free to amend or consult it as needed to meet your needs. You can write down the terms and phrases that you are unfamiliar with. To motivate yourself to study, you might also write the explanation or description of the phrases or words you have gathered. Writing down your notes is crucial if you are reading with the intention of learning. When you first start taking notes, you'll see that you've gathered a lot of superfluous words—far too many words to use in your notes. You ought to edit it when you've determined this. To get better at taking notes, you'll need to practice.

Generally speaking, your notes should have two different kinds of elements. A few noteworthy quotations, succinct paraphrases, or summaries might be included. You may also discuss how the material made you feel after reading it. After

CHAPTER 15: SPEEDWRITING FOR FASTER NOTE-TAKING

reading the content, you can select emotional responses and questions based on how you're feeling. For taking notes, you may utilize a variety of formats and styles, including linear, diagrammatic, and pattern.

- In a linear system, headings and subheadings are used to provide logical flow from one section to the next.
- When using a diagrammatic system, you may navigate the website with the help of the flowcharts and boxes.
- When it comes to the pattern system, mind maps are a great way to organize a lot of information into one space, but you'll need to take memory and retention skills into account.

It is up to you to decide on the style while taking the needs and conditions into account. An additional crucial component of taking notes is practicing summarization. A summary aids in keeping important details together. It also elucidates the author's primary point of view and reasoning. The nicest thing about a summary is that it's written in your own words, and you may use it as a reference in the future and within your field of study.

You ought to review your note once you've made it for the first time.

It will assist you in creating an ideal synopsis based on your feelings and responses as well as the language that surrounds the papers. To divide up concepts, you might utilize various sheets. You may use colored pens or flags to draw attention to specific areas, and you can use various colored pens for different themes. Additionally, you have to explain why you changed the note.

Considering the situation, you can gather a large number of

notes. Your notes will be meaningless and a waste of time if you gather them without considering the necessity or significance of what you are collecting. Thus, it is imperative that you take notes in an orderly fashion. The tools you choose to take notes will determine how organized your notes are based on your needs. Which tools will be utilized for taking notes may depend on your particular preferences. But one of the greatest ways to remember and preserve information based on your needs is to take notes.

CHAPTER 15: SPEEDWRITING FOR FASTER NOTE-TAKING

Note-Taking for Verbal Exchanges

Taking notes is crucial if you anticipate needing to review the explanations in certain circumstances. Not only is taking notes crucial when attending a conference, meeting, or preparing for a speech, but it's also crucial to document any topic presented for any given circumstance or purpose.

Making notes will enable you to pay close attention to what the speaker is saying. Active listening is a necessary part of any note-taking method if you want to capture the significant points that will come up later for various uses.

These goals could have to do with your career, studies, or other pursuits. It is necessary to know what note-taking tools to use for meetings, seminars, and other events if you wish to take notes in an orderly manner. One of the most basic and easy methods to take notes is with a pen and paper.

Common Guideline for Note Taking

It's important to be clear about your goals when you first start taking notes. You ought to use your note as a roadmap for your learning and development in light of the incident.

You should determine if the point is worthwhile to add in the memo.

You can occasionally take notes on new terms. You ought to stay away from the topics that have previously been discussed regarding a term. It is important that you focus on the main ideas that are discussed in the text.

Use your own words and adhere to your own style. When taking notes, there's no need to consider spelling, grammar, neatness, or punctuation.

You will intuitively comprehend the significance of your notes when you read them later. With practice, you will become more proficient and advanced in the note-taking process.

Using bullets or numbered lists according to your needs, you must make an effort to keep your writing to a minimum and stick to the required word count. It facilitates connecting the dots between thoughts or ideas in the text. Short forms and abbreviations are also acceptable.

A highlighter pen can be used to underline or circle words or phrases to draw attention to their significance.

You may put in place a structure that you will eventually comprehend.

You shouldn't freak out if you forget something important.

Once the events are over, you should go over them again and make any necessary revisions. If you find that there are any gaps in the notes you took, you can review them.

The Cornell Method is one option if you want to take notes. You may use this useful technique to split a notepad page into three sections: a recall area, a summary area, and a note-taking area. The bottom portion should be considered a summary area, and the left margin should be considered the recall area. We'll write notes on the remaining portion of the page. If there are any gaps in your notes, you should write them as soon as the event has occurred. There should be some white space between the notes' two points. It is advisable to select keywords for each significant topic. These are the terms you need to stay in the recall area.

The summary section should contain your summary. Color coding is a useful tool for locating certain areas. You can create pertinent notes later on when you check the summary section. Students that use this note-taking strategy to prepare their lectures before a test stand to gain the most.

Tips to Take Notes More Effectively

To ensure that you study and comprehend any subject in accordance with your needs, you must adhere to a few crucial guidelines when taking thorough notes.

Being able to take notes is crucial for success in the workplace, in business, in the classroom, and in other contexts.

- **Make Arrangement**: It is advisable that you read the suggested text's background information before taking any notes on it. If there have been any prior notes on the text, you should review those as well. It will assist you in gaining an understanding of the general format of the notes pertaining to the recommended subject. As a student, you have to go over the theme on the syllabus and take notes on any recommended chapters to gain an insight.

You should bring the necessary tools and come early for your meeting, class, or conference. You won't have time to gather the necessary note-taking supplies if you are running behind schedule and neglect to bring a notebook or pen. You can also experience difficulty focusing.

This will prevent you from gathering all the necessary data and will also cause a rift among the other participants.

- **Listen to Understand**: Taking notes requires you to comprehend the subject matter, which is crucial. Your ability to listen well will aid in your comprehension of the subject or information. You'll be able to focus more intently and quickly take in all the relevant information and keywords. You will also benefit from being able to recognize tone variations, expressions, and other particulars that the lecturers utilize to communicate clearly. These are the most important things to include in your notes. You will be able to discern the relationship between various points made in the speech if you are an attentive listener. You must ask a question to get your questions answered if you wish to learn more or gain an understanding of the subject. Your notes will be very beneficial for reviewing or revising in addition.

- **Select only the Essential Part**: Every word in a speech has the same importance. It is up to you to decide where best to take notes based on your needs. In most speeches, just a few points are crucial. You will need to use your own analytical abilities to describe the main ideas.

The speech's remaining sections cover expletives, audience participation, and answering questions.

identifying the key ideas and providing an original explanation of them. If required, you should also include subheadings. When you are pressed for time, you may condense your notes by using short phrases or symbols.

- **Maintain an Organized Note**: Applying lovely accents or patterns is not necessary when taking notes. Sustaining a regular degree of structure will aid in your comprehension of the message. To make your note more precise, use headings, bullet points, highlighting, subheadings, and so on. When taking notes, you should also utilize symbols and acronyms. When taking notes, make sure you have enough paper to write down any thoughts you have about the lecture. If diagrams, mind maps, or flow charts are required to make sense of your thoughts, then go ahead and utilize them.

When you use a mind map for a certain subject, you can relate to it, which aids in determining.
- **Review Thoroughly**: One of the greatest note-taking techniques is the Cornell Method, and going over your notes is beneficial. It is not required to rewrite notes if you use the Cornell Method for taking notes. You can save time as a result of this. You'll find it easier to understand the speech's concepts thanks to your thorough notes. The review section allows you to write the main points in your own words. When you reread after taking notes, the information will be easier for you to understand and your notes will help you remember it. You may effectively summarize the topic by using the review column's collection of important concepts.

16

CHAPTER 16: WRITING SPECIFIC DOCUMENTS

By now, if you've read every chapter up to this point, you should have a general understanding of how to get better at writing and reading. It is now necessary for you to acquire the skill of writing certain papers that you will require at every stage of your life.

Writing a CV or Resume

It's imperative that you write a Curriculum Vitae, CV, or resume if you want to be hired. This is an essential document that you will be bringing to your prospective job, thus it is crucial. It is essentially a very thorough paper that lists all of your greatest accomplishments, abilities, and credentials. It also lists any prior work experience you may have had. In contrast, a resume is shorter than a CV since it provides all of this information in a more condensed style. You may think of it as a condensed version that emphasizes the accomplishments and abilities pertinent to that specific position or opportunity.

So, I'm going to provide you some advice and fundamental guidelines so that you may create a flawless CV without making any mistakes. Selecting a format is your first duty. You can get them online in a variety of formats, but as you read this part, you'll learn a lot of new information. Make sure to include your contact information at the top of your resume. Your address will come after your name at the top of this. Add your phone number and email address as well. You should choose your CV's typeface wisely. It ought to be simple and uncomplicated. It ought to be sufficiently readable for all users. 11-point typeface size.

Next, you must include your most important qualifications, accomplishments, expertise, training, and job history. Each of these parts will have a different length, which is mostly determined by the kind of job you are looking for. One thing you must keep in mind while formulating the accomplishments is that you should only address issues that have previously arisen and for which you have already offered a remedy. Put your focus on the result and the work you did.

Consider everything that is pertinent to the position for which you are seeking. If you believe anything should be addressed, bring it up right immediately.

It is useless to include every strange job you completed during your final summer of college if you already have work experience; but, if selecting any legitimate experience is also required, then go ahead and list the jobs.

Even if you've taken a lot of courses, it doesn't matter because you only need to mention the most highly relevant ones. The resume that your daughter has should be free of typographical or grammatical problems. It ought to appear polished and unambiguous. Furthermore, resist the urge to lie because your employer will undoubtedly find out.

Writing a Cover Letter

You will also require a cover letter for your job applications.

A cover letter serves as an introduction to you and a showcase for your qualifications. Ultimately, a call to action is required since the letter should motivate your employer to review your CV. However, the cover letter shouldn't be very lengthy in this instance either. Generally speaking, it's best to write a new cover letter for each job application. If you don't, your lack of initiative will be apparent in the generic tone of the cover letter and will come off as lazy, which is not a good first impression for your company.

Finding out to whom you are sending the cover letter is the first task you must undertake. Some individuals choose to write "to whom it may concern," however this is not the proper method to send something. It will make a greater impact on the person if you are able to get their name. Most of the time, if you are applying based on a job post, there will be a name listed that you must send your application to. However, it is usually preferable to address someone by their last name or by Mr. or Ms. Never use their first name.

You might attempt calling the individual if you know who to contact and you have their contact information in order to get further information about the position. You should find out if you will be working in a team, what kind of person they are looking for, and if they have a position description, among other things. These responses can be extremely useful in framing the replies, so make sure to write them down.

It must include your contact information at the top. While providing your postal address is not required, providing your phone number and email address is. If your job application is for an organization that is situated overseas, don't forget to provide your country code. You will also need to state your desired job. You will next check that your abilities align with the job description. You must also include a succinct explanation of your qualifications for the position. It's a benefit if you can communicate with the parties involved in the same language; don't forget to include this in your cover letter.

There shouldn't be any grammatical or spelling mistakes. Verify the name of the firm you specified is accurate. Since the main focus of a cover letter is on how you might benefit the business, try not to place too much attention on the first person. One further common error that individuals do is to state that they are applying to other jobs. You are, of course, as nobody applies to one job at a time, but your cover letter doesn't need to address that.

Writing a Personal Statement

A personal statement can be applied in a variety of situations. It can occasionally be used for your resume as well. However, the end goal is the same regardless of the use: you are attempting to market your abilities in the most in the most persuasive manner conceivable. Your personal statement must therefore be unique. In this competitive environment, this is what will make you stand out from the throng. These personal statements may occasionally be needed when submitting admissions applications to various universities. Writing a strong personal statement could mean the difference between getting hired or not. So, take care when you write it.

A personal statement should ideally be no more than 150 words, however if If you're writing it for your resume, it can be three to four lines long. Don't waste this precious space talking endlessly about your abilities. You need to be succinct, precise, and memorable. You must keep in mind that this is really a brief synopsis of your cover letter and not your resume. The specifics can be covered in your cover letter at a later time. It must be relevant. A strong personal statement will address a number of issues, including your aims and aspirations, what abilities you can provide to the firm, and who you are as a person.

If you are having trouble coming up with ideas or finding something to write about, look at the job It's usually a good idea to describe.

Another option is to start by writing a draft without any word restrictions. You can edit and condense the text once you've finished writing it for your personal statement. Take your time with the process. You have plenty of time, as your personal statement is quite important. It is undoubtedly not something you will come up with in a few hours because, on occasion, condensing everything into such a small amount of space might be the most challenging aspect of a job application. You have to sound both sophisticated and authoritative at the same time. Thus, choosing the right words is crucial. Given the short time of the personal statement, you should concentrate only on your advantages. The first line needs to be intriguing and unexpected. Don't try to overthink things because the ideal introduction will strike you at any time.

Your personal statement should be a reflection of your unique voice and personality.

You shouldn't be projecting an incorrect impression of who you are. Additionally, you must always speak with honesty. You and your identity are the subject of your personal statement. Put an end to copying others and start expressing your own thoughts instead.

It is possible to have it reviewed by another person who will also proofread it, as occasionally new information becomes apparent when reading from an alternative perspective. It can also be read aloud several times, since it frequently aids in emphasizing points that require adjustment. Reading the work aloud will assist you in determining the issue if there is a lack of coherence between the paragraphs.

Writing a Report

The fundamentals of authoring reports were previously covered in Chapter 6. I'll be giving you some more advice on the subject right now. When writing reports, it is always recommended to use names and pronouns. Consequently, you may employ "I, me, he, she," and so forth. Words or phrases like "this person" or "the above-mentioned person" must be avoided. There are persons you may encounter who may claim that using impersonal language in reports increases objectivity, however it is untrue.

Avoid being awkward when expressing your opinions. There should only be one concept per sentence. Straightforward, brief words save others time because they are easy to read. additionally, they require less complexity. Simplified sentences save time, so if you put yourself in the position of the person reading the report, you'll see why I'm saying this. Furthermore, inappropriate lengthening of sentences often results in errors and needless stretching of the sentence.

Try using nouns at the beginning of your sentences to keep the syntax simple.

This makes the procedure simpler. Longer sentences require more complex punctuation, which increases the likelihood of errors. An additional consideration for you to make is how many commas you use in a given sentence. There need to be just three. The sentence will grow more complex the more commas you use. Additionally, be sure you are not ambiguous when your explanations. Everything needs to be precise. If you want your report to be flawless, you must aim for clarity.

Aim to limit your discussion to visible facts and avoid conjecture and gut feelings.

These items should not be included in a report. You must provide facts, not conjecture or sentimental statements, as they will not hold up in court. All of the material must be arranged into distinct paragraphs. This will improve the overall logical flow of the report and make it simpler to read and comprehend.

Only use the active voice; the passive does not represent objectivity.

Make the right numbering of your bullets. This increases the clarity of the information you are presenting.

Writing to do a list

To-do lists have been around since the beginning of time because they make life so simple and easy to handle that you can just keep checking items off the list without having to think about anything else. Most people in your immediate vicinity will admit to using a to-do list at least once or twice in their lives if you ask them. Individuals frequently worry about unfinished tasks and worry that they will miss out on significant events during the day. Our minds prefer things to be organized and completed. Because it keeps everything in front of you and eliminates all other worries, that is why having a to-do list is so beneficial. But this is the finest guide for you if you're not sure where to begin.

You can make several lists if you are the type of person who frequently forgets things. You can make two lists: one with tasks that must be done whenever you have time, and another with tasks that must be finished in a set amount of time or within a specific period of time. Short lists should be made of the tasks that need to be finished within a specific amount of time; otherwise, the list won't appear doable and you'll start worrying again. Each list serves a different purpose. The first list's objective is to serve as a reminder of all that needs to be done at some point during life. To make it easier for you to look at everything at once, try to confine this list to one page. The second list is all about priorities and how you should direct your attention toward the items that are most crucial. This will guarantee that you are getting everything done while your energy is at its peak, which will increase your productivity.

Additionally, you can make weekly or daily lists. If you are making a list every day, it ought to be doable. Limit it to three or four things, but don't let that stop you from doing more. You can, of course, but keeping the jobs smaller will increase your confidence, and you can always choose another activity from your weekly list and finish it if you think you've finished it. Lists that are excessively lengthy can cause worry and defeat the whole point of making to-do lists. Your lists must come to an end before you will feel satisfied with your accomplishments. Larger activities can be divided into smaller phases, such as micro-goals, if they need to be finished. Your ultimate life goal will be reached through all of these smaller objectives. If you have to file a tax return, for example, you can divide the procedure into manageable phases that will simplify the process rather than

CHAPTER 16: WRITING SPECIFIC DOCUMENTS

just writing it down. Your lists ought to be maintained current. For the following few days, you must update your lists to avoid becoming stranded someplace. Make sure to leave room on each list for any last-minute, urgent tasks that may arise.

Set priorities for your chores and give them a deadline if you have to complete so many in a day that you are losing track of them.

In today's environment, these lists have become an essential part of daily existence.

Writing a Letter

The audience and type of letter you are writing have a big impact on the format of the letter. A casual tone will do if the letter is addressed to a close friend or relative, but if it is meant for a formal

for professional goals or business dealings, in which case the format and tone will also be different. The details that are displayed in the upper left-hand corner are your name, city, street address, state, and zip code. After that, you must insert a line break and the date that the letter is being written.

You then have to write the recipient's complete address after skipping one more line. Information such as the name of the recipient, the company, as well as the mailing address, must be stated. The section where you write the greeting follows. The salutation is another name for this. You can write Dear in informal correspondence, but Sir or Ma'am are more appropriate in formal correspondence. A general "To whom it may concern" will also suffice. After that, you must begin the letter by skipping one more line. The letter's body shouldn't be awkward and should only have one paragraph. There must be several paragraphs, and each new notion or concept must be covered in its own paragraph. Steer clear of technical jargon in casual correspondence. Only use them if the person you are speaking to is aware of them. what you are bringing up. Keep the letter to a maximum of two pages and avoid making it too long. Formal letters require you to be exact and concise.

There should never be threats or defamation in a letter, not even when it's a resignation or complaint letter. Two of a letter's most crucial sections are the introduction and conclusion, which

CHAPTER 16: WRITING SPECIFIC DOCUMENTS

need to be handled properly. While you can close informal letters with a personal note, formal correspondence needs to be written in a more formal manner. You must make your argument quickly and avoid digressing into unneeded topics. As quickly as possible, you must state your letter's purpose. The letter's wording ought to be kind and civilized. Regardless of your anger against the other person, you should still speak politely. Since formal letters must be more accurate, length plays a role. It must not be extended beyond what is required.

When you have to explain your reason for leaving in a resignation letter, things can get very confusing. You should not include in your letter the fact that you were having trouble getting along with coworkers, your supervisor, or other people if it was the reason for your resignation. It is entirely up to you whether or not to disclose any personal reasons for your resignation, such as a possible career change.

Your correspondence ought to be printed and, ideally, signed. Additionally, you ought to provide an invitation to your manager to stay in contact with you even after you quit. You can keep the door open by doing this. To make the transition easier for the business, you may also suggest someone else to take your place. Additionally, you can provide your assistance in reviewing the applications from outside applicants. It is advisable to send your letter at least two weeks before your resignation date to avoid surprising the employer with an unexpected absence.

Between your complimentary closing and your final paragraph, there should be a space. A complimentary closure is a way to express appreciation to the person who received the missive. Since "sincerely" can be employed in a variety of situations, it's generally a safe bet. However, you can also use "cordially" or "warm regards" if you and the recipient of the letter have a cordial and friendly connection. You will find a number of more possibilities if you conduct some online investigation. A comma must follow every complementing closure. The only letter in the phrases that needs to be capitalized is the first one. There should be a few spaces before your signature, which must be placed last.

Your name should be typed in full, in business letters, behind your signature.

CHAPTER 16: WRITING SPECIFIC DOCUMENTS

Composing Powerful Emails

Professionals now use emails exclusively, and I'm sure you can't envision a day without receiving at least one. However, not every communication will provide the outcomes you were hoping for. What then is the fix? The techniques you employ and the way you apply them to your writing are what hold the key. Office workers are said to receive 80 emails a day on average. Because individuals receive so many emails every day, individual messages are frequently missed. You must bear these suggestions in mind if you wish to prevent your emails from getting missed.

Don't ever communicate too much

An individual's overwhelming amount of emails received at work frequently causes worry and tension. Therefore, you should consider whether or not it is truly required before responding to an email. Furthermore, bear in mind that sending communications by email is not always the safest option.

On occasion, people forward emails without deleting the discussion history. They may wind up disclosing critical information that they weren't supposed to in this way. Additionally, you ought to make an effort to avoid sending critical or personal information by email.

Good subject lines are essential.

Have you ever read the news and felt the headline was uninteresting? You'll notice that news stories with attention-grabbing headlines will draw you in. The email subject lines have a comparable function. The opening sentence should both immediately capture your attention and explain your main points. Never leave the subject line blank in an email since the recipient will more likely ignore it or put it in their spam bin. It is advisable to include the date in emails you send to someone about weekly or daily projects so that you can stay on top of the task.

Speech should be succinct and unambiguous.

Like formal or professional letters, your emails must be succinct and to the point. The content of the email should be clear and informative, and all relevant information should be included. Moreover, you should write several emails for each concern you have rather than cramming all of your questions and concerns into one. It's also important to find a balance and avoid sending too many emails to one person. Use bullets and divide material into manageable chunks if there are many points that need to be covered in a single email.

Be courteous in your wording

People frequently overlook the fact that emails are just electronic versions of old letters, thus they must be formal and courteous. Your email's message has a significant impact because it clearly conveys your degree of professionalism. Even when you get along well It is best to steer clear of slang and colloquial language when speaking with someone. Inappropriate abbreviations must also be avoided. Emojis can be useful at times since they can help to make purpose clear in specific contexts. It's possible that your recipient will decide to print your email and forward it to others. Thus, the language you choose is quite important.

Checking the tone is necessary.

In order to fully comprehend someone when you speak with them face-to-face, you need pay attention to their facial expressions and conversational tone. However, since emails lack any visual or aural clues, you are cheated out of this chance. Nothing should be unclear or contain any ambiguous language.

Proofread

To ensure that there are no errors, proofread your email before clicking the "send" button. There shouldn't be any typos or errors in grammar or punctuation. Similar to how what you wear to work represents your professional image, the recipient of your email will likewise get a sense from it. People don't like long emails, therefore it's important to pay close attention to how long the email is. Make it brief, but remember to include all the information that is required.

Conclusion

We appreciate you reading "Accelerated Learning Techniques: How to Improve Your Study Skills and Learn Anything Faster" all the way through. Optimize

Your comprehension and speed reading skills. Let's hope that "Smart Analysis & Information Synthesis" was educational and able to give you all the resources you need to accomplish any and all of your goals.

This paper's theme is really straightforward: effective study techniques are necessary tools that must be acquired and put into practice.

These abilities are very beneficial in all facets of life. "Accelerated Learning Techniques" encompasses a broad variety of competencies, such as time management, conducting research and evaluating verbal and nonverbal communication, listening, and creating brief notes. or taking, in addition to additional activities that enhance and fulfill the learning process.

What type of learner a person is at this moment is irrelevant. If individuals adhere to the straightforward advice presented in this paper, they can do tasks more quickly, effectively, and stress-free. Recall that falling behind in your coursework is the main source of aggravation for college students. Students who take charge of their time and assignments can overcome that problem rapidly. To put it another way, the goal is to complete tasks with extreme accuracy and focus. being aware of when and exactly what to do. With these pointers at hand, the student will instinctively know that "Just Get It Done" is the most important advice of all.

In the end, a learner with strong study techniques will be more competent, clever, self-assured, and successful in both their personal and professional life. It is believed that by giving

CHAPTER 16: WRITING SPECIFIC DOCUMENTS

readers and learners in general access to this knowledge and ideas, they will become not only more productive students but also more capable leaders.

Applying each of these techniques to your own life is the next step.

Reading more will benefit you in two ways, so put it into practice. You will learn new terms that will expand your vocabulary and improve your writing abilities in addition to improving your reading comprehension. After reviewing the fundamentals, all you have to do is You will advance to a higher level if you practice. Naturally, it will take time to become an exceptional writer; nevertheless, if you are willing to study and try new things each day, I guarantee that by the end of the month, your writing abilities will have significantly improved.

While you're reading and writing, don't forget to proofread your work because all of your hard work will be in vain if it's riddled with spelling and grammar mistakes. I've even included some advice on drafting some of the most common documents that we need in our daily lives in this book. If you are writing them for the first time, draft them first to check if you are satisfied with the way they turned out and proceed to frame the completed version after that.

WRITTEN BY
GRACE TAYLOR
THANK YOU
THE END

www.ingramcontent.com/pod-product-compliance
Lightning Source LLC
LaVergne TN
LVHW021047100526
838202LV00079B/4610